DREAMERS &
CHANGE MAKERS

23 Inspirational Stories From Women With A
Vision For How We Can Change The World

PINEAPPLE PUBLISHING

Dreamers & Change Makers

23 Inspirational Stories From Women With A Vision For How We Can Change The World

Published in the United Kingdom

Curated by: Chanel Morales

Cover & interior design by: Michelle Catanach

Published with the support of:

TEAMAUTHOR UK
Publishing with you

This book is dedicated to all the dreamers and change makers doing small things to make our world a better place.

Foreword

Hey there Dreamer! You made it!

Welcome to the book that's been created just for you.

We are here to show you how any woman who dreams of a better life has the power to make it happen. And how you too can become a leader of positive change in the world.

I hope this book finds you well, but also at the perfect time. Just as you're considering what you really want from the next chapter in your life; we are here to guide and inspire you, to give you ideas and prove that no matter where you are right now, anything is possible.

The idea for this book came to me one night just as I was drifting off to sleep. I have always been a dreamer.

Always half imagining a better world and honestly believing that I had the power to make it a reality.

Never one to settle for anything *just the way it is*.

Always believing we can do anything, create anything, live any way.

But I knew in my heart that I wasn't the only one. I knew that the Dreamers and Change Makers of the world needed a voice. I knew that there were so many women out there doing small things that had a huge impact, and that together we could create great change in our world.

The general narrative goes, that in order to make a difference we must have great power and great wealth. Within these pages, I'll be sharing with you the stories of how twenty-three very ordinary women from around the world have started a movement to create positive change, and how you can too.

We are the dreamers and the change makers. We are the women who would not settle, will not stop and are no longer silent. We have a voice, we have a vision and now we have the chance to share our ideas with you.

I hope you enjoy.

Chanel x

Contents

From Broke Single Mum, To Six-Figure Business Owner: The Secret To Creating A Life Of Freedom & Happiness

By Chanel Morales

There are many things I have seen in this world that I have wanted to change. But the one that inspired me the most and the thing I truly believe made me the change maker I am today happened to be the first.

I was twelve years old the first time I visited my mother's home country. Peru was beautiful, breathtaking and magical to me in so many ways. The people, the colours, the food, the mountains. I'd never seen such rich culture or mountains so tall.

But alongside the beauty was the poverty. I still remember when a little boy, who must have been about eight years old, came up to our table in a restaurant. He had no shoes on and limped on a clubfoot, with his little sister trailing behind him. He held out an empty plastic bag and started speaking in Spanish and pointing to his mouth and then down to the bag. I realised he was asking for us to scrape our leftover food into the plastic bag for him. My scraps. For another child's dinner. I cried and cried.

It was genuinely a life-changing moment for me. From that point on I realised how blessed I was to be born where I was. And from that moment on I wanted to understand why we can have such an abundance of food and wealth in the west when there is such poverty in other places. Why some people, even in my own country, had so much when others had so little. Who or what decides this? How can it be changed?

I wanted to do something to make the world a better place. I was twelve so I didn't understand any of the politics or the economics of it. All I knew was, it wasn't right that half the world lived that way when the other half lived with waste and abundance.

I am pretty sure it's one of the reasons I've never been a big worrier or complainer. My friends always comment on the fact that nothing seems to bother me. Well, this is why. I mean what is there to complain about? REALLY? If you live in the west you have an abundance of freedom and opportunity, so much that you can never really understand.

This memory has been with me for many years. And as I grew up, of course I began to understand more of the complexity of the problems we face in the world. It's not as simple as giving our food to those in poorer countries. It's about opportunities, education and many other economic factors. But one thing that has become clear to me in recent years is how mothers have such a huge role to play in this.

When women and mothers especially have money, they use it to feed their families and do good in their communities. When women have money, the world is a better place. And yet in so many parts of the world, women don't have their own money and don't have the same opportunities in education or in making money.

At nineteen I became a mother myself. My ability to provide for my daughter came from the fact that I was lucky enough to live in the UK. I received state benefits, housing and support for childcare. At twenty-one, I went to university. I received funding for tuition being lucky enough to live in a country that supports higher education.

And I am reminded of that every time I think about that little boy and his sister and wonder what their mum must have been going through for her kids to be begging on the streets.

It is pure luck and chance that we are born where we are. And that is why I feel so passionately about the importance of raising up everyone in the whole world. I have a big dream. For women from every nationality to be able to support themselves and their families financially.

But all big dreams start off small. They start with the very first step. One of the things many women who want to do good in the world forget. A very important lesson in creating change. Fill. Your. Cup. First.

As a single mum working in a job I hated, I had neither the time, energy nor finances to create change much bigger than myself. So, I started there.

When I got my first nine-to-five office job in 2015 I knew instantly that it wasn't going to be for me. Working for the man was nothing but boredom and misery. Missing out on time with my daughter, commuting and working for just enough money to get by. I remember looking up at the clock on the grey wall, and looking around at all the miserable depressed faces, wondering if that would be me in twenty years.

That was not my idea of an amazing life. My idea of an amazing life was to travel the world, enjoy time with my daughter and be totally, unapologetically free.

Yet there was no clear answer from anyone around me as to how I could achieve this. No one knew what to say to me other than that 'this is the "real" world now'.

Being the dreamer I am, I of course never settled for this answer. I started on my own journey of discovery. I uncovered a whole new world of freedom and opportunity: women who were world-schooling their kids; single mums travelling the world; families living in campervans and off-grid communities.

It was at this moment I realised that the voice inside my head telling me that I had to get out, that this wasn't the life for me, wasn't madness! In fact, it was my soul telling me what I needed to hear. *Have you ever heard a voice deep inside your soul telling you that something isn't right?* Yet we dull down these sounds with TV, social media, alcohol and drugs, constantly distracting ourselves from our internal guide.

This realisation for me was life-changing. The realisation that I could have the things I dreamed of. That a life of freedom and fun was really possible. I just had to figure out how to get there. How were these women and families doing it? How did they support themselves financially whilst living these amazing lives? I soon realised that there was one answer: online business.

At first, my goal was simply to replace my nine-to-five income with something I could do from home. Escaping my job was the number one thing on my list of dreams. I started researching into online businesses and soon discovered a black hole of scams, pyramid schemes and network marketing companies.

I wanted something different. Something totally unique and totally mine. I wasn't going to sign up for an MLM company, I didn't want to sell someone else's overpriced products. Why was it so hard to find something real? No wonder people are so sceptical of online business.

Over the next few months, I spent every waking moment researching online, downloading all the free PDFs, webinars and tutorials. I started to see a clear pattern of what would make me real legitimate money and what were just fake funnels and scams.

Like most dreamers, everyone around me thought I was crazy; my family thought I should just focus on moving forward in my career. My friends thought I lived in la-la land. My boyfriend didn't understand why I was spending so much time "working" and making no money.

But I knew that the first step to having an impact on the world was to sort out my own world first. As women, we so often forget this very important life lesson. When you are happy, healthy, successful, and fulfilled in life, everything else falls into place.

We so often associate doing things for ourselves as selfish. But when we become the best version of ourselves everyone around us benefits. There were nights when I sat up on the laptop ignoring those around me. There were definitely times when my daughter sat on her tablet longer than she should have so that I could work.

But the drive for me was so much bigger. The freedom to have control over my own life and have the power to do good in the world was so important to me, that I couldn't stop. I had a vision that no one else could see, and that's okay. Not everyone needs to understand where you're going as long as you do.

After a lot of time spent at the computer, I did eventually figure things out. I started freelancing as a social media manager and had the very wobbly foundations of a real business. It was only a few months later that I got made redundant and my boyfriend and I broke up.

This for me was the biggest turning point in my life. I remember walking out of my job for the last time, with a skip in my step, so over the moon to be let go with two months' pay. I drove home, in the summer sunshine with my window down and the warm air blowing on my face. I just knew this was the start of something amazing.

The break-up wasn't such a fun experience. As you can imagine, the end of a three-year relationship is always going to be hard. But there had been something missing and the adventurous spirit I always had wasn't something we shared. I knew I would have to do something big to shift the feeling of sadness.

Sometimes I wonder where I'd be now if those two things hadn't happened at the exact same time. Two huge negatives to most people turned out to be the making of me. Would I still be working in that job, hating my life? Would I still be in a relationship, in one place with a mortgage, a dog and a two-week holiday every year?

The big thing I decided to do, to shift my low mood, most people thought was crazy... giving up my social housing, selling all my stuff, taking my daughter out of school and booking a one-way ticket to travel the world. All with no savings and relying solely on my freelance income.

Our first long distance flight was booked on such a budget that the eight hours from London to Boston we had no TV screens or even free water on board. The flight cost just £150 though, so I guess you could say you get what you pay for.

We made it from Boston to New York, New York to Philadelphia and Philadelphia to Washington DC all by the skin of our teeth. I'd be waiting to get paid by a client so we could book our next bus or train or Airbnb. It was enough to even stress me out! And not much stresses me out.

By the time we reached Austin, Texas to stay with another single mum I'd met online through one of the travel groups, we were both exhausted. This long-term travel business was not what I thought it would be. It was draining, hard work and stressful.

I was running my business, freelancing for others, writing tonnes of social media content whilst promoting myself at the same time, home-schooling Nyneave, sightseeing and moving from one place to the next every few days. I realised whilst sitting in the hot Texas sun that something had to change, I couldn't go on like this.

Although freelancing is a great business model, it's time-consuming and not scalable. To make more money, you have to work more hours. This wasn't what I signed up for. I wanted more freedom, not more work. Once again those around me went back to the same old narrative; if you want to be successful, you have to work hard... and that's what most people genuinely believe.

But I listened to the voice deep inside me that told me there had to be another way. Once again, I started to research and read. It was around this time I discovered that not all businesses are created equal. Some businesses take more time, some businesses are more scalable, and some businesses are nothing but hard work.

We landed in Hawaii to be greeted by another amazing world-schooling family at the airport. Katherine and her little boy were our hosts and we spent five amazing days exploring the island. On the first day, I said to myself, it's time for a rest, it's time to wind down and have a break from social media. Hours later I dropped my phone into the sea... an accident caused by the Universe. Be careful what you wish for.

I then had time to reflect and detox in the most beautiful place on Earth. The downtime showed me once and for all that my intuition had been right all along. Rest is just as important if not more important than work. Working hard will only get you so far. Downtime is essential to success.

It was in Hawaii during this downtime that I found my inspiration again. I went from working hard, working more, lacking any kind of vision, inspiration or joy, to being full of ideas once more. And that's why I always say when you feel you are lacking motivation, when you are overworked and achieving nothing, you should stop, have a break and a digital detox. Working more and working harder is not always the answer.

My ideas started flowing and I began to see that all around me were other women wanting to travel with their kids. Inspired by my journey and my photos, they wanted to know how I was doing it.

I created The Dream Club on a scrap of paper in my bedroom in Hawaii, the twelve steps to starting an online business that can give you freedom. I knew how to get started, I knew how to make money. I knew I could help other women like me do the same.

But starting out as a coach wasn't as simple as it looked. I had a number of failed launches before I had any success. Most people don't talk enough about the failures but I like to share them. I am not perfect and the business I created isn't either. In business, you either succeed or you learn. My talent is jumping in with both feet and then picking myself back up when I fall and carrying on.

In the end I realised that I couldn't do it all alone. I wanted to be a coach but I'd never had a coach myself. So, in 2019, I hired my first coach, then another, then another. They taught me things I'd never have learned alone. They showed me things I would never have known I didn't know.

Then 2020, the year the world went crazy, was my best year in business. And that's the thing about the online world... It's just not as open to disaster as other types of business. You have an international economy, international opportunities, so success is almost inevitable if you have the right attitude and consistency.

It was 2020 and that was also the first year I made 6 figures in my business. And I don't tell you this to brag. I tell you because I want you to understand that the only difference between you and me is consistency.

I don't work harder than anyone else, I work approximately three days a week. I'm no smarter than anyone else, I just focus on learning the things I need to know to make more money in less time. **Anyone else** can learn these things.

But the truth is I don't need a six or seven-figure business to enjoy my life. I loved my life before I made a lot of money. Happiness is not in alignment with our income (past a certain point). I am happy because I am so free. So free and in control of my own destiny. I am happy because I am doing my own thing, not playing to anyone else's tune.

Of course, it's an amazing feeling not having to worry about money. I have been broke. I have been in debt. I have relied on state support. It's an amazing feeling being able to buy whatever you want without looking at your bank account or stressing that you might end up overdrawn.

But money isn't the goal. The goal is freedom. The goal is impact. I'd never be motivated to make money in my business so I could pose with designer handbags or fast cars. I'm good so long as I have my pineapples.

I strive to grow my business because I know that when good people earn more money, we have more power to do good in the world. One more dollar in my pocket is one less in Donald Trump's! Empowering women to make money from anywhere in the world, no matter their circumstances, no matter how many kids they have dangling off their arms!

Creating an online business gave me the freedom and opportunity to completely change my life. From a broke, single mum in debt to six-figure business owner. And that's why I'm so passionate about sharing it with others. What I know could change the lives of so many women. It already has.

For me, business is about so much more than my livelihood. When I coach women to start online businesses, I am teaching them skills that will help them to provide for their families. The women I coach then go on to create massive impact with their businesses and the ripple effect is never-ending.

I have always felt passionate about supporting developing countries and now I am in the position to do so, which feels amazing. I honestly believe that with words we can change the world. We first change people's thoughts and ideas. Once those have shifted, we will start to see action and impact.

So, what is the secret to creating a life of freedom and happiness?

Freedom: Firstly, define what freedom means to you, then create a plan to make that a reality. Physical freedom? Sell all your stuff and go. Financial freedom? Create an online business, pay off your mortgage, invest in stocks. Emotional freedom? Get rid of the negative people in your life, get therapy, deal with your demons. What do you need to do? Everything is possible.

Happiness: Choose to be happy, it is a choice. You can choose to focus on what you have, on the beauty of the world, of the opportunities in your life. Choose to put yourself first, yes, *you* must fill your cup first, do what is right for you, even if you are a parent. Choose to do what sets your soul on fire. Listen to the voice inside your soul that tells you to do the crazy thing and trust that you know what's best for you, no one else. You only have one life and holding back will never leave you feeling satisfied. And finally, do good things in the world, give back in some way, even if all you can afford to give is a smile.

All the women in this book have something important to say. Having created massive change in their own lives and the lives of people around them. Together we are creating a real impact on the world. I hope as you turn each page you are inspired by our stories and feel inspired to change your world, and then the rest of the world in any way you can.

About the Author

Chanel Morales is the Online Business Coach for women who want to change their life by becoming an online entrepreneur, so they can make a high income from home, or wherever they are in the world.

Chanel has spent the last few years launching multiple successful online businesses and developing extensive marketing and business expertise.

Chanel is the founder of Pineapple Publishing and The Dream Club which is her signature group programme helping women get from employee to entrepreneur in 12 weeks.

In 2016, Chanel realised she wanted more from life. More time with her family, more money in the bank and more freedom to travel. Sick of working in a 9-5, making someone else rich, she entered the world of online business.

The businesses she created gave her the freedom to quit her full time job and spend three years travelling the world with her now 11-year-old daughter.

Chanel's current primary focus is on helping other women to generate a high income online so that they can create the lifestyle of freedom and abundance they crave.

Website: www.thedreamclub.co.uk

Facebook Page: www.facebook.com/mumbiztravel

Facebook Group:

www.facebook.com/groups/digitalnomadmums

Instagram: www.instagram.com/mumbiztravel

Email: chanel@thedreamclub.co.uk

Here's Your Sign to Start Living Purposely

By Natalia Cerain

Natalia,

Hey, Honey. It has been over fifteen years since we have actually sat together and spoken. Beyond fifteen years, really, since you've opened your heart to me and really allowed yourself to feel vulnerable to all the joys and tribulations you've gone through. Since our last speaking, you have found and lost love, achieved education, buried loved ones, and gained a baby. You have obtained the American Dream that they all said you should strive for, and all before the age of thirty. It wasn't your dream, but hey, you achieved it. It only cost you your physical health, your mental strength, your second child, and overall, your happiness. I suppose we can touch on all of that in this letter, but I'll start by saying we should really talk more often.

So, let's revisit, shall we?

Right after high school, you received a scholarship to go to college. You already had a couple of years' worth of college credits upon graduating, so time away in college was rather short. Rightfully so, because you hated it. There wasn't a group of people you fit in with. Which didn't bother you, really, because you never truly fit in with any one group before. You got along, but never really settled in amongst anyone in particular. While away at school, you lost your first love. Maybe distance was the culprit. Possibly the idea that you were changing into a different person. But whatever the cause, your breakup led you to the relationship that brought you your daughter.

Having your daughter was an emotional whirlwind. Of course, the typical fears any mother has when they first find out they are expecting were constantly jumping through your mind, but also the outside stressors put another layer of terror into the mix.

Do you recall the Spring of 2011?

Standing at the foot of her hospital bed, the stench of the medical-surgical unit wafting into her double-bed room did nothing to keep your pregnant belly calm. After just coming from the emergency room, everyone, as a family, finally had enough space to sit and digest the new diagnosis of lung cancer. Your grandma. Little Lady, as you sometimes called her when feeling playful. Standing at 4 foot 10.5 inches (don't forget the half), she was a dignified woman. Short in stature, but mighty in presence. Her words were often few, but when she spoke, the room listened.

May 16, 2011. A Monday. The day after she missed your college graduation. You, at first, were upset with her because she said, "just a little pain", is what kept her from witnessing her eldest granddaughter walk across the stage. You came to learn it was uncontrolled pain that brought her into the emergency department. Watching her losing the fight against drowsiness as her pain meds kicked in plunged a knife deeper into your heart. The stoic woman you knew your entire life was slipping away.

You, your mother, her brother, her sister, and your newly-showing seven-month baby bump made the small room crowded. An awkward silence settled as everyone sat adjusting to the new situation you all knew needed to be faced in unison. Your uncle, the jester of the family, never missed an opportunity to poke fun at someone, and you were the easiest target, always willing to take the bait.

"So, when are you and Jim Bone getting back together? The least you could do is listen to me since you're about to pop that thing out," waving his hand aimlessly towards your belly.

It's a well-known fact, the meaner your uncle is to someone, the more love he has for them. The only one who never needed to question your uncle's affection is your ex-boyfriend, who your uncle lovingly renamed Jim Bone. No doubt, an amazing guy, and there were years of a loving relationship, but the relationship ended with no prospects of rekindling after you moved away. And definitely not with the baby on the way which certainly wasn't his.

You elected to be a single mother. You knew very well who the father was, that was never a question. Although he certainly was not the family's favorite, you were not looking to return to a failed relationship solely to satisfy some kind of social standard for motherhood.

"James and I are friends. That's all. We'll stay friends. But I'm not looking for a baby daddy just to appease you. If you're still in love with James, Uncle, maybe you should reach out to him." You all laughed, trying to invite any lightness into the room. Just as quickly as everyone roared with laughter, a hush came upon the room as Little Lady sat up and adjusted herself to speak.

"James respects you. And you respect him. There will always be love there. But when something in your life isn't working for you, you give it the boot. Kick, kick..." Her little size four foot could be seen under her blanket animating her words.

These were the last words of advice that she planted within you. Advice that you often find yourself referring to, even to this day. Although your Little Lady passed away just shy of your daughter turning six weeks old, she knew the blueprint to the journey ahead of you. She also elected to be a single mother to her three children. Rather than settling, she chose to put her children before marriage. She decided to utilize the village of family to help raise her kids. Like every new mother, you were scared shitless, but you had that same village to help raise your own little one.

At one point, you used to imagine being stopped at a fork in the road, pondering for a little too long over which decision to make. You can hear the uniquely raspy voice of the Little Lady, highlighting your options, but never telling you the answer. And for the longest time, an answer is what you were always on the hunt for. Never the typical *what's the meaning of life* type of questions. No. Sometimes you just wanted simple guidance to tell you to go left or right.

Over time, you decided that the fork in the road was truly just one lane that offered limitless opportunities to you. So instead, you'd ask, "What in the world am I doing here?" or "Am I going along too fast? Too slow? Am I missing something?"

Not in the destination, but in the journey is advice you'd remind yourself of but never really listen to. Your journey through your life. At times, you would bebop along, moving ahead blindly and trusting your feet to move on their own. Other times, you'd stubbornly park yourself on the side of the road and just rest for a period only to later determine you've rested too long. But never did you turn back. You couldn't.

But let us continue...

Less than six weeks after introducing a new life into the world, you laid to rest a grounding force so pivotal in your life. You were angry? Hurt? Lost, perhaps? You had no idea how you felt besides guilty for every feeling and thought you had concerning your grandmother's death. Though she secretly knew she was sick long before she told anyone, it wasn't until she was given her prognosis of less than three months before she shared any news. You took ownership of her decisions. You felt like you didn't do enough to help her help herself.

The Little Lady was a woman who calculated all her actions before taking them and needed a damn good reason to sway her mind. But you felt nothing but sorrow that you let her down. You should have been able to recognize her pain, her deterioration. Just months prior, you had taken the Nightingale Pledge. Learning you couldn't change someone's mind, even to save themselves, was a hard lesson that took you a great deal of time to learn. Both with your patients and with yourself.

Being a couple months postpartum of your first pregnancy, you didn't know if the dread and despair you felt was the result of passing a new life through your body, or something more. You certainly didn't think to check in with yourself. You didn't think to share your feelings with anyone else. You utilized none of your outlets and didn't think to look for one. In your mind, if you were able to stand up straight and produce enough milk to feed your newborn, you were contemptuous. So, of course, that's when you lost your ability to stand up straight. Literally.

You couldn't take more than two steps without looking like you downed a bottle of whisky on an empty stomach. You couldn't stand straight; your equilibrium was gone. You ignored all the signals your body sent your way until you couldn't avoid it any longer. It scared you enough for you to take your underweight butt to your healthcare provider. With your physical assessment turning out uneventful, your nurse practitioner turned the visit into a psychosocial visit.

"Are you sleeping?"

"I have a newborn," you offered as an excuse. True. But you're that mom that says you have the perfect baby. (And rightfully so. After her first month of getting acclimated to her new world, your little one slept for twelve hours every night with only a mild stirring when she needed to have another shot of milk, then she would be out again.) Also, at this time you worked nights in twelve-hour shifts and stayed up all day with your baby.

"Any thoughts of wanting to hurt yourself?" your nurse practitioner asked.

"Myself? No. Never suicidal thoughts, only the occasional homicidal." So glad she got the joke.

"Has your appetite changed?"

"I eat when I remember. Often, I only remember when I notice my milk supply changing. But I have started to set notifications on my phone to remember to eat and drink."

"Any changes or stressors with work?" she continued.

"I'm a nurse."

"Understood," she chuckled. "Any recent traumas? Deaths? Relationship?"

"Well, just my grandmother, about five months ago. I helped take care of her before she passed. And about six months before she passed, her brother - one of my favorite uncles - passed. And before him, a total of six other relatives at various times throughout the past year."

She flashed a sour look on her face, one that said oh, honey….

"Well, you don't realize you're depressed?"

"…Say what now?" Your thoughts started firing.

Depression? How the hell did she come up with depression? I've never been depressed. Sad, yes, but not depressed. Nothing I'm going through is anything abnormal for a new mother… right? Right! I'm a mom. A selectively single mom at that. I'm young. Educated. Black! I treat depressed patients, not get depressed myself! Besides, I swear I don't even have the time to be depressed. I mother. I work. I shower. I sleep. I repeat. Every day is clockwork. I clearly function without missing a beat… I purposely designed my life this way. Robotic, so to put minimal thought towards my day-to-day routine. I wasn't depressed. I couldn't be. I have patients who have depression, not me. No time for that… Right?

After four and a half seconds of fighting with yourself, you finally looked up and met the eyes of your nurse practitioner. Every thought you had must have been etched on your face because you could see the pity radiating from her eyes. Pity not for your diagnosis, but for the fact that you were clearly trying to rationalize your way around this new information. All you could do is close your eyes and sigh.

"No. I didn't realize I was depressed," you conceded. "How does your assessment conclude that?" You were slightly annoyed with yourself. But mostly embarrassed.

"Equilibrium disturbances are a symptom of depression. Situational Depression, more specifically in your case. Step back and think about it, Natalia. You already know you don't have to stay in bed crying all day to be depressed. With your recent history over the past year, you've been through a lot. And you haven't given yourself the time to process and cope with so many life-changing events all at once. I want you to go see a therapist. A person on the outside to help you process."

Well, damn. There it was. The wakeup call you needed to come back to reality.

Name it. Accept it. Move through it.

She was undoubtedly right and you knew it. Your job was to assess psychiatric patients routinely. Since completing clinicals in nursing school, you have always considered yourself a psychiatric nurse at heart. You absolutely loved it. A hundred people could have the same diagnosis and you'll get a hundred different presentations of symptoms at any given time. Be it schizophrenia, depression, borderline personality disorder, addiction; you're forced to look at, treat, and interact with each person as an individual. They each bring their own traumas, their own triggers. Their own human element. And for you, professionally, nothing else could top that.

You pride yourself in teaching others to understand that everyone has mental health, just as they have physical health. An individual's level of "healthy" fluctuates with any given circumstance. Recall the examples you give patients; catching the common cold or having a broken bone. Even experiencing an emotional loss like a death or joyous celebration like a wedding or birth. They all affect your health, good or bad. You've preached this to hundreds of patients, families, and even geeked out to your professional peers who didn't have the same respect for psychiatry as you do.

Why couldn't you extend that same respect towards yourself?

Well, by this time you've taken all self-care out of your life. Your world revolved around how much you could give to someone (everyone) else. How much could you ease another's suffering. You'd take on the emotional burdens of those around you and neglect yourself. No more walks out in nature or just spending time sitting in the sun. No more loud music to reset your energy or letting your body take over in dance. And nothing of your most powerful act of self-care – taking pen to paper to force yourself to see your emotions reflected off the page.

But, I digress…

You went to see a therapist, as ordered. A psychotherapist, to be exact, which specialized in family support and counseling. You were referred to a white lady, on the better side of middle-aged, with no children and supposedly left home right after high school. She was so far removed from your personal realities that the eight weeks of sessions proved more burdensome than beneficial. Yes, she initially offered the opportunity to voice your woes, but after the second meeting, she made it clear she was not going to attempt to connect with you and took more time thoroughly dissecting the "where you went wrong in your life was…" side of your story.

"Your baby is beautiful but, if you hadn't decided to be a single mom, then you could…"

"If you decided to work in a hospital rather than a psychiatric forensic prison, then you would have…"

"If you would just let yourself cry and feel your pain, then maybe you…"

No effort is needed to determine when you're on the receiving end of being shamed. It's one thing to lay it all out in a journal entry - or to anyone who can relatively relate to you, for that matter - but to pay a professional to berate you for thoughtful choices you were proud of, that's an entirely different beast.

You stuck out the remaining appointments, but after the paid mini-trauma sessions with that therapist concluded, you, at last, did take the time to focus on yourself. Having a name for the fog you were in you helped and you were able to handle yourself with a little more care. Not too much, just enough to make it through your day with enough mindfulness to walk straight.

As you like to say, time never heals things, you just learn to cope. Days muddled through into years. You laughed, genuinely, throughout those years and let yourself feel and cry when you needed to. You felt as though you learned to better prepare for the situations that sent you through highs and lows.

Your family; the welcoming of new babies and the celebrations of college graduations.

Your career; the progression from staff nurse all the way to Director of Nursing.

The material; buying your custom-ordered luxury vehicle and building your dream house all before the age of thirty.

But the more you achieved, the emptier you felt. And you knew it. Yet still, you did nothing about it until your body threw you off your journey again, forcing you to sit down and have a think.

Although you didn't turn to me, your trusted journal, that's okay, I'm sure you can recall the exact moment that I'm speaking of now - when your world stopped cold.

The time when you've been so hurt, not on a physical level, but an emotional level. So shattered, you wouldn't doubt what you felt was also on a spiritual level. Hell, whatever you want to call it, you never felt pain like it in your life.

The miscarriage of your son has been - and still is - a terrifying reality that has been unmatched by any other. Going from the high of hearing a heartbeat and seeing a little pea on the ultrasound screen to, less than a month later, finding a faint streak of blood after using the bathroom. Then having an ultrasound tech nonchalantly telling you, "Well, it was so early, you can always try again."

True, you did lose your baby "early," as the ultrasound tech oh-so-gracefully reminded you. You were ten weeks along. Too early to buy a new crib or plan a baby shower, but ten weeks deep into a new and extraordinary love affair that your heart was wholly invested in. A bond that you, even years later, may find yourself in tears over if you let your mind wander too far.

Most of the in-betweens weren't relevant enough for your memory to retain. Just snippets of that emergency room visit. You at times can recall how your body went cold the instant you heard the words, "…no heartbeat…" uttered to you in the exam room. Since you wear all of your emotions on your face, that ride-of-shame you took on the stretcher as you were transferred back to your emergency suite reassured you that everyone in that emergency department knew the news of your lost baby, before you even had the opportunity to process it.

How does someone even prepare themselves for such an event? There's no mantra you can utter enough times to alleviate that heartache. You're still in search of the proper journal prompt to express the dismay and grief. Does every woman feel the same level of embarrassment, violation, even?

Violation, not because you were stripped down just to your hospital gown, bra, and rainbow knee-high socks. And you surely didn't feel embarrassed for the vulgar names you secretly called that ultrasound tech for the heartless way she handled delivering the news of your miscarriage. Not even close. Your embarrassment and violation came from the shame you assigned to yourself. You let yourself fall in love with your little boy (and yes, you were certain he was a boy, just like you were certain your daughter was a girl, even that early in your pregnancy). You allowed yourself to fall in love with the adjustments your body was starting to make. The gas, the nausea. The running to the bathroom every twenty minutes. Even the tight-fitting pants caused by the slight swell in your womb. You welcomed all of it! But you needed someone to be at fault for taking this joy away from you, and the only logical person to blame was yourself.

You worked too hard during the day.

You stressed too much during your master's degree program in the evening.

You didn't sleep long enough at night.

All of these emotions were so immense that the whole world could clearly see it, but only you could feel it. Although you still had your loving village embracing you, you felt completely alone in this event, so, back into your depression you went. You let yourself sit there for a little while, too. And rightfully so. You needed to feel this pain. For once, you acknowledge that your pain was real. That's an improvement for you. You laid in bed, only getting up when necessary. You decided to forego using tissues two boxes in and settled on rotating your pillow whenever the spot you were laying on became too saturated with tears.

In order for you to move, it took your daughter -then only seven years old and purposely kept in the dark about your early pregnancy- asking you, "Are you going to get out of bed or are you just going to lay there for the rest of your life?"

There it was again. That reality check.

You had a blessing, literally staring you in the face, asking you to get up and live your life.

Forget the fancy car and the smell of fresh paint in a new house. Who cares about the hard climb up a career ladder? You can even forget about the hours on a yoga mat and your gym memberships. If you're willing to allow your mental health to go uncared for, nothing in your life will align properly. If your daughter didn't remind you that you had so much right in your grasp, who knows how far you would have let your mental health slip. Physical health, interpersonal relationships, and material things can and will easily dissipate if your mind isn't right..

I won't review the hardships of your body physically letting go of your baby six weeks after the miscarriage, nor your emergency surgery for internal bleeding the following year. It goes without saying that it took you a few more lows before you committed yourself to stay on the right track of protecting your mental wellbeing.

Your story has been in the works for the past thirty years. You have seen so many others like you - mom, nurse, single woman - running through life on a hamster wheel, trying to check off the generic list-to-success that society has plotted out. Chasing dreams that were never your own has led you down paths that literally cost you your mental and physical health. Unlike you, so many don't get the opportunity to change their life. To decide to live actively, purposefully, and presently in their lives.

If the more "successful" you become, the more you are left feeling empty, depressed, and desperate to rewrite the past years of your life, then you need to redefine success. Think back on the times you felt pure joy and pride in your decisions. How empowered did you feel when selecting to be a single mom? You were floating on air when your hard work to pass your nursing boards on your first try paid off! You were even walking taller when you could afford to have your daughter in the private school of your choice.

Take the Little Lady's words into account. If something doesn't work for you, give it the boot...kick, kick. Only you can live your life, Natalia, and you've learned the hard way that you don't do well when you don't nurture yourself; your mental health.

It's a cliche, but life really is a journey - a straight line, even - from beginning to end. There are no forks in the road and there is no reverse. There will likely be no one to tell you the answers you may want, either. You'll have to chart your own map. But know that, as you stay in your lane, you have to keep trekking on. Pullover when you must. Hell, park it when you feel it necessary and ask for help. Just hold on to the fact that everything you have passed along the way is as it should be.

As you and I have been reintroduced, I look forward to a new narrative of health and adventure. Crank up the music and wind the window down because you have a way yet to go. Move in purpose and take care of yourself, then will your light be bright enough to shine for others.

Forever your ally, Natalia,
-Your Journal

About the Author

Natalia Cerain is a Registered Nurse, educator, and lover of *tell it like it is* conversations. The change she is working to see in the world involves providing education and awareness so one day mental health is taken as seriously as physical health.

With over ten years of experience as a nurse, Natalia has experienced a lot of different personalities and her goal has always been to have a positive impact on every patient and client she works with. She has worked in various healthcare specialties, including forensic psychiatry and hospice, and over the years she has seen time and again that honesty and transparency is best when working with people and their health.

As an educator and a single mom, Natalia is dedicated to filling the gaps in health literacy by providing factual, unbiased, and much-needed information that empowers you to make optimal decisions for your own health. With her science-based education and Piscean spirit, she sees no limits to the possibilities and success of her clients.

Email: Natalia@NataliaCerain.com

Dance to the Beat of Your Own Drum

By Julie Beck

I have now reached a stage in my life where I no longer believe we should settle for just getting by. I now embrace freedom, growth and most of all, permission to be my true authentic self without worrying about how it will all come together. It's not an easy path to take, as it can often go against how society and even those closest to you expect you to behave. We are, however, in a much better position than our parents and grandparents were in. There is a much greater awareness and acceptance to be different and individual, yet many are still fearful of taking this path. Often the road of least resistance can seem like the easiest option, where you can easily hide from your deepest fears and blend in with the crowd. Social validation of how you live your life is never going to make you happy. It may seem acceptable to begin with, but often when there is personal growth you begin to question why you are existing in this way. Many relationships break down at this point, as it seems that you are behaving irrationally or you have seemingly 'changed'. In most cases, you are evolving into your true self and peeling off the layers of conditioning that you have abided by for so many years. Could we possibly view the phrase 'a mid-life crisis' as a cry for help where people have stood up and said enough is enough? I'm not suggesting for one minute that you abandon your responsibilities and disappear off to a desert island where you can meditate for eight hours a day searching for your true calling. It's about creating balance in your life and taking small steps to uncover who you really are and what has led you to question your current life path.

Do you ever question why you work so many hours just to get by? There has been an acceptable obsession, in more recent years, with working to the max and filling our diaries with social engagements. Even our children have a busy calendar. When does that leave time for you to rest and recharge? Perhaps you question why you are saving all year for a holiday, only to return back to work feeling exhausted and frustrated for another ten weeks. Did you choose your career path or did you end up where you are now in order to impress or please others? Perhaps it was the promise of a moderate level of income that caught your attention or knowing that you are paying into a pension to create financial stability for your future. The truth is, we can't fully predict what will happen and how safe our investments are. I have heard people say that they won't go for a promotion at work because it will bring more stress and push them into a higher tax bracket. Why would you increase your stress levels for a slight increase in salary? Is it because that's just what you do in order to be successful? Is there an alternative way to view success and not to presume that our main source of financial abundance should flow from our current salary alone? When you live from month to month with no savings or alternative income streams, the pressure to keep going can be quite overwhelming. Let's not even discuss how retirement looks if you are hoping to live comfortably from your pension alone. At this rate, a lot of us will burn out well before retirement age. We are not meant to operate like a machine; we need to grow and evolve. Yet when the ego is the driving force within our own decision-making we can lose our connection to source. Sometimes we may need to dig a bit deeper in order to find our true purpose in life.

The world has experienced some crazy times recently and there is certainly a push to create financial abundance through alternative sources. I'm not suggesting that you join some dodgy scam for a quick fix. The solution is far simpler yet for many quite a difficult process. Why? It is based on your own internal belief system and years of social conditioning. If you have believed there is a limit to how much you are worthy of earning and the ways in which you can earn it, I can happily tell you that you are wrong. If you are stuck in a rut, you need to listen to the nudges you are being given. Do you dream about doing something completely different or do you keep seeing adverts or receive emails about opportunities that seem interesting yet a little alternative? Start by asking yourself:

- Do you find joy in being creative and using your hands?
- Do you enjoy being outdoors and connecting with Mother Earth?

- Do you feel drawn to healing and inspiring others?

You are never too old to learn and definitely never too old to earn from a career change.

Let me take you back a number of years. I had always felt there was a way to exist on a deeper, more spiritual level. I have always felt a pull to visiting churches to gather my thoughts and try to connect with a higher source. Only now do I feel comfortable in saying that I am not a religious person, nor do I identify with a particular faith. My true inner faith is purely in connecting with a higher source and with those who want to raise the vibration of the earth and live life with an open heart. It is also very important for me to connect with those who also have this vision but are not sure how to make it happen. Living in a state of wellness and inner happiness can only be created and embraced by YOU! In virtually all of my career roles, I have adopted a wellbeing approach to how I work with my colleagues and customers.

It wasn't until I entered my forties that I felt confident enough to launch my business Holistic Heart Wellness. I wanted to create a path that I could explore and expand in at my own pace, learning all of the time. I know that this is my life purpose and I am excited for what is yet to come. I am very fortunate to also have a career with a company that values every single employee and is passionate about making a difference in the world. If you want to make changes in your life but feel a little overwhelmed, I'd urge you to connect with organisations that share your core values. This could be employers or manufacturers. Be mindful of where you shop and what ingredients are contained in the products you purchase. There are many companies that aspire to be a 'B Corp' classification, which means they put the planet and people ahead of profit.

In the last few years we have seen a move away from a strict set working pattern. Dolly Parton's hit song '9 to 5' highlights how times have really changed. The routines that our parents adopted may seem a little old fashioned now. I can remember my mum would have dinner on the table within minutes of my dad arriving home from a full day's work in the office. Then thirty minutes later my mum would head out to work and dad took over the childcare duties. This was seen as a normal way of life for a lot of families as I grew up. It's only in more recent years we have begun to question why. As companies pushed for equality in the workplace, women were given opportunities the previous generation had only dreamt of. The only major hurdle females faced was how they would combine a career and motherhood. Thankfully we have supportive employers that encourage you to return from maternity leave and often accept reduced or flexible hours. I personally still feel there is a huge pressure on women to be a provider, carer, partner and yet still hold time to be their authentic self. Roles in the workplace have become more flexible and combining inclusion and diversity at the forefront, there has never been a more opportune time to go for a career of your choice. If you have found your dream job, then it is very well done. If you live for the weekends and get that sinking feeling on a Sunday evening, you really need to think about how long you can sustain this path.

We are out of balance and seem to have too much pressure on the mind and not enough physical activity. In the past, there was a wave of manual jobs that involved a certain level of physical fitness and durability. As we have technology at our fingertips and we have the option to work and play 24/7, we have to be disciplined in defining our boundaries or we could burn out. When we rely too heavily on technology, we can find that our creativity is suppressed. The younger generation have grown up surrounded by technology and find it difficult to imagine a world where our main form of communication was once from a landline telephone.

Electromagnetic pollution (EMF) can be quite overpowering. We have so many devices in our home, we may be quite unaware that this can be draining and interfere with our own energy balance as well as our environment. All devices are surrounded by their own energy field. When we are in close contact with these devices for long periods of time, it can leave us feeling drained, experiencing headaches and insomnia.

Has artificial intelligence (AI) led us to new technological heights? It allows companies to predict what consumers will do next and can track your data from personal technology. You are encouraged to use the latest app or download software to help save time and give you more control over your life. My question is, are you really in control or are you being controlled?

We are surrounded by so many people who want to give back to the world through important roles such as doctors, nurses and teachers. However, these roles often leave people trapped in the vicious circle of stress from the immense pressure of working such long and unsociable hours. They are in a very difficult situation as they want to inspire and support people on their own journey, but the restrictions placed upon them can be quite overwhelming. So many talented people have left these professions due to stress, unhappiness and not being able to spend quality time with their family. The education sector is under immense pressure to produce a certain standard of performance from each student. The majority of teaching staff have their own unique gift to bring but often don't have the opportunity to let it shine due to following strict guidelines within the teaching curriculum. I do feel that schools offering mindfulness and meditation as part of a daily timetable will create a hugely positive effect on how the young people of today will cope with their decision making in the future.

I think we have to have an open mind as to what is now deemed as an acceptable career path. Gone are the days where the only option if you wanted to be successful, was to follow a profession, for instance, a solicitor or doctor, to carry on the family business. No wonder so many people were deeply unhappy. They followed a path that they felt they should follow, not because they actually wanted to. If they didn't follow a recommended route they would be viewed as a chancer, unreliable and possibly an outcast to their family and the local community. The younger generation could be at the tipping point of a stress and depression epidemic. We need to support and encourage them to preserve their vision and more simplified view of the world before they are sucked into the void of technology, comparison and materialistic pulls. Stress could now be the modern-day silent killer. Short term or acute stress is perfectly normal; we need this to kick-start our fight or flight mode, a natural survival instinct. There are controversial theories that highlight living with continued levels of stress can lower your immune system, leaving your body more prone to diseases such as cancer. Our ailments and sickness records are increasing. Perhaps our bodies are politely nudging us to slow down and look after ourselves more. Why are we so quick to opt for over-the-counter remedies or prescribed medicine? Have you ever stopped to observe the natural remedies at our fingertips? Crystals are the jewels of Mother Earth. They are believed to contain healing energy. I have often been asked, 'what if I can't see the benefit of a crystal?' I explain that you can't see love but you know it holds great power. Crystals vibrate at a high and stable frequency that can help to balance our energy that has become sluggish or blocked.

Crystal therapy treatments are an ideal way to cleanse and reset your energy. You can also quite simply pick crystals that you are drawn to and carry them in your pocket or wear healing crystal jewellery. On a personal level, I use Lepidolite for when I can feel my mood start to dip. It is known to be beneficial as a mood booster and also help support those suffering from depression and high levels of stress. Crystals can also play a great part in absorbing electromagnetic pollution. Try to place some crystals in each room near to WiFi points, electrical sockets and laptops. There are many crystals that are believed to absorb electric and magnetic fields (EMF). Shungite, smoky quartz and green aventurine are just some of the many suggested crystals to place near devices; they are also beneficial to have in our pocket. Just remember to cleanse crystals regularly, there are lots of simple ways to do this and are easily found online. My preferred method of cleansing crystals within my home is with sound. I have a bell that I use to release any stored energy from the crystals.

Reiki is a healing technique based on the principle that the therapist can channel universal energy to activate the natural healing process. Homeopathy is a holistic medicine which uses highly diluted substances that have the main aim of triggering the body's own healing mechanism. It is based upon the theory that 'like treats like'. Aromatherapy uses aromatic plant extracts and essential oils for healing. There are many other complementary and alternative healing practices. If you have not looked into this area I'd urge you to at least find out more. Our own internal healing system is very powerful but sometimes we need some assistance.

I wonder if more people tried alternative and complementary therapies that medical intervention could be avoided? Let's look back in history. Many ancient civilisations used crystals at the heart of their communities. Were our ancient ancestors aware of something more powerful? Perhaps greed and power now motivate our civilisation, thus leading us to lower our energetic vibration and connection to source.

Our bodies are affected by our thoughts and emotions. The power we have over our own body is much greater than you may think. How many of us put 'me' at the top of their to-do list? If a friend or family member said they were feeling under the weather, I'm sure the majority of us would offer our services and ask them to slow down and rest. We are naturally caregivers and we feel compelled to help others. If we continuously deprive our bodies of self-care and love, then we are not filling up the energy tanks. Over time they will deplete and we will receive warning signs as we plummet towards the reserve tanks. Unfortunately, if we do not heed the body's warnings, we may cause disease to manifest from the negativity and stress that we constantly surround ourselves with.

When was the last time you walked barefoot on the sand or even on the grass? Have you ever sat out in the moonlight and bathed in the beautiful energy? Connecting with the earth is such a simple way to keep you grounded and recharged. I love to visit the beach and watch the sunset. I find this such a powerful way to be grateful for the opportunities of that day and to relish in the natural beauty that surrounds us. For some of you who don't live close to water, spending time in nature can be just as rewarding. I always find a powerful way to take in the moment is to be aware of all your senses and thoughts.

Mindfulness is now a common practice and can really help you to process the here and now. So many of you will live your lives by schedules and reminders. Have we really become so busy that we need to block out time in the diary just to relax? How often do you practice genuine gratitude? This is very much linked to whether you have a fixed or growth mindset. Having the latter means you are open to learning and developing and can often cope better with obstacles. Life itself is truly a miracle. There are many opportunities surrounding you but often you can't see them.

Your general outlook could have been formed during your childhood or from the support network that surrounded you. When you are faced with the knocks and hurdles that life presents to you, often you can begin to lower your expectations of deservingness. Your self-worth can take a knock and you can begin to accept this as your path.

Living in a world of a 'lack' mentality is very detrimental to your mental wellbeing. Sometimes it is difficult to determine where this acceptance of lack originated from. It can come from various sources, including our ancestors and past lives. It is more commonly recognised as connected to childhood experiences or from negative relationships.

We are all made up of energy and like attracts like. Everything around us is energy too, even static objects such as a mug or chair. If we think negatively and focus on a bad experience, we are very likely going to bring more negative situations into our path. If you choose to see obstacles as just a learning curve and view your life as pretty awesome and full of exciting opportunities, then guess what will happen? You are creating a frequency that the glass is always half full. We are influenced by our current domestic situation, families and friends. Past lives and the behaviours of our ancestors can also play a part in how this life flows.

It is believed that genes passed down from our ancestors can hold patterns of behaviour that we are influenced by. There are many theories about whether our soul is reincarnated many times in order to experience and learn important lessons in each lifetime. If this is true, could past life energy and memories also be filtered through to the next incarnation?

Our body has chakras and meridians that are conductors of energy that flows throughout the body. We are also surrounded by an aura that is often known as an energy field. When the energy flows freely within and around us we will operate at a higher vibration than if we have energy blockages. Energy cords are energy attachments that can link us to others, situations, ancestors and even past lives. When we are not aware of these cords, we can often stay stuck in the same mindset; we may find ourselves struggling to move on from a previous relationship or the loss of a loved one.

During history, we have seen waves of female-dominated energies followed by male energies. There has been a huge surge of feminine power in more recent years throughout developed countries. Sadly, some more remote and controlled states have not seen a shift in the balance of energies. I do wonder if the 'independent woman' status may have been taken to the extreme on some occasions. In order to sustain a harmonious world we must blend our energies to create balance. There seems to be a huge increase in the last decade of people worldwide developing life-threatening diseases. There still, however, seems to be pockets of civilisations and communities that buck this trend. Could it be that they are living a simpler life that allows them to feel free and in control, using the natural resources that surround them? Don't get me wrong, some communities where living off the land that they inhabit can be extremely hard work, especially when natural disasters can leave them cut off from the world. Yet somehow, they look content and connected to the earth and all its hidden treasures.

If this resonates with you and you want to take back control of your wellbeing and connect more deeply with the natural resources of the world around us, I'd love you to join my free group. There you will be part of a supportive community of like-minded people and be able to access a free downloadable wellbeing document. This highlights the main core areas of your life and how making small adjustments can make a huge difference creating more freedom and boosting your energy. Shine your light brightly and enjoy the journey.

About the Author

Julie Beck is a Spiritual Wellbeing Coach, who combines her passion for crystals and energetic connection with more mainstream wellbeing coaching. She relishes the exploration of spiritual viewpoints, alternative healing practices and how to reconnect with Mother Earth. Coming to the realisation, a little later in life, that we may be more in control of our destiny than we once thought, Julie is currently following the law of attraction principles. She helps clients to focus on mindset and the belief that they are deserving of success, good health and happiness, which can play a huge part in their overall wellbeing. More recently, Julie has transitioned into offering online wellbeing support and short courses to help clients find their work/life balance. Combining previous experience within career guidance and wellbeing, her organisational skills as a PA and her empathic nature, Julie is a natural at coaching clients. She is passionate about helping others to find and shine their own light brightly and to follow their soul path.

Facebook Page:

www.facebook.com/holisticheartwellnesscommunity

Facebook Group:

www.facebook.com/groups/holisticheartwellness

Email: info.holisticheartwellness@gmail.com

Recreating Our Reality: How to Level Up from Merely Existing to Living Extraordinarily

By Naomi Beverly

"Is something not working for you? Change it. Do whatever it takes for as long as it takes. Save yourself. Tap into the Divine, clarify what you want and manifest it. All of it!"~ Naomi Beverly

A Bit About My Story

If the year 2020 taught me nothing else, it is to be grateful and thankful for everything. Our world can change in a heartbeat. It also demonstrated the power of following my dreams and the magic of manifesting. The levity of letting go of that which no longer serves me. The magic in facing my fears so that I can taste the freedom that awaits on the other side of my manifestations.

What a seismic shift the entire planet has gone through! Some people lost everything - their lives included...and others had the most profitable, most amazing year of their lives. Did mindset have anything to do with why some people were focused solely on surviving while others were able to thrive? The answer, in my humble opinion and experience, is an overwhelming and resounding YES for the majority of instances. Mindset is key. But there is more to it.

And I am in no way discounting the external factors that impact our lives. They matter. As a veteran classroom teacher with over a decade of experiencing how millions of things that are outside of my control affect outcomes and student performance, I'm equally convinced that holding myself one hundred percent accountable for making the best of whatever IS within my control is the ticket to transformation. Our mindset is one hundred percent within our control. If you are open, I would love to share with you what I've learned in this area that has helped me along my journey.

I am thankful that I have been able to transform my life from where it was to where I am now. I started off life born to parents who married, created two children together, and quickly went their separate ways after divorce. My sister and I stayed with our mother and my other half-siblings in New Jersey, while my father moved "down south" to the Southern region of the United States of America. For a few years, we bounced around from place to place; my maternal grandparents' home, my paternal grandparents' home, apartment after apartment, and several times I was sexually violated. I didn't tell anyone until much later in life.

However, before my father had moved, he promised both my sister and I that he would get a house for us and then come back to get us so that we could live with him. Which he did. By the time I was seven and for reasons unknown to me, a court of law signed over full legal and physical custody of my sister and I to my father, and we moved "down south" with him. Shortly after, he remarried, and we lived together for a few years with our stepmother. But they, too, divorced.

By this time, I was a preteen and missing my mother terribly. Unfortunately, she was facing significant challenges with addiction, so although my father had promised several years earlier, that when I was thirteen, I could go live with her. I soon found out that I could not...and I was traumatized.

Devastated.

Destroyed.

There were times that I had gone two or three whole years without speaking to her or even hearing much mention of her. It's kind of like she just didn't exist, although she was on my mind every day. Sometimes at school, I would just daydream about the day I could be with her again. I started experimenting in many of the ways that teenagers experiment.

During that time, despite being surrounded by people who loved me, I felt as though I never really had anyone who *truly* cared about me...which wasn't the case. I was loved and valued. This is an example of feelings not being facts. My father always made sure that I had women as role models, such as my godmother, and a close family friend (who, to this day, sends me birthday cards without fail). My dad was *incredibly* involved in our lives. I was extremely close with my counselor at school, Mrs. Lonnie Austin. She would invite both my sister and I over to her home for the weekends sometimes just because she could see that we needed a little bit of extra love! We would go shopping, or to the movies, or just hang out and talk. My favorite person on Earth at that time was my high school coach, James "Friday" Richards, who also took us under his wing. But Coach Friday took *everyone* under his wing and loved all of us students and athletes for about forty years before he passed.

And, during high school, I had *the most phenomenal* boyfriend ever. He was the captain of the football team and he was absolutely my best friend and closest confidant. One of the kindest guys you would ever want to meet. We ran track and field together, spent all our free time together, and I went to both my Junior and Senior Proms with him. He had his head on straight, and his positive influence kept me out of a lot of trouble. He was definitely an angel sent by God, and I am blessed that we are friends to this day. I went on to earn a full track and field scholarship to college, graduate, earn a Master's in Mass Media, and I have just completed a Masters in Instructional Design. Yes, studying, sports, and being surrounded by positive peers and loving parental guidance have been critical to my success.

I realize now, however, that not being able to accept love is a trauma response, and I've put in a lot of work to undo all of the deeply rooted beliefs that I had subscribed to as a result. I focus my studies on social emotional learning, and I help others write about their trauma as a tool for healing and rebuilding their lives. In my case, being separated from my mother (whether it was for my own good or not) and feeling abandoned by her left a gaping "mother wound" that would shape and influence my relationship with myself and other women for decades. I am happy to report that we have a close relationship now. I can and do call her whenever I need someone to lend an ear. I absolutely love my mom and I am thankful for her recovery, her grit, her strength, her resilience, her perseverance, and her courage. I am grateful that the Divine saw fit that I would come earth-side through her vessel.

Furthermore, it affected my chakra alignment, specifically my root chakra and it has taken years for me to feel safe enough to even want to put down my own roots. Additionally, I was unconscious of the notion that my thoughts about myself as being unworthy or undeserving of love influenced what I expected and projected into the world... and then, of course, my world became just a mirror of my thoughts and beliefs. It was a cycle that I am happy to declare and decree is broken. I now practice the steps of bending reality at will, and I am in the process of perfecting it to manifest the life of my dreams. There are still pieces that I am working on getting how I'd like them to be, and I put the work in daily to make sure that it happens.

The Start of My Transformation

In 2018, I embarked on a journey of continual expansion and personal growth. I have sought to understand my life from a deeper, more spiritual perspective. I have sought to widen my perspective and understand my journey as part of a larger, cosmic, multiversal, timeless, energetic, and more collective experience than we are typically indoctrinated with in Western society.

Consequently, over the past few years, I've been exposed to wisdom that crosses physical and temporal boundaries. Wisdom that intersects science, religion, spirituality, culture, and tradition. Wisdom that is not restricted to what we humans experience with our five senses alone. Wisdom that has been around since the beginning of time. Also, the most exciting part for me is that I have barely even scratched the surface of what there is to learn.

The lives and realities that our amazing minds can conjure and manifest when we learn to bend reality by accessing altered states of consciousness is phenomenal, miraculous, and extraordinary. What I am happiest to report is much of the "magic" is duplicatable. There absolutely is a process - which when paired with strategies and tools that we can learn, access, and implement - will catapult us in a quantum leap toward transforming our current reality into the life we truly and deeply desire.

Four Levels of Consciousness

I learn from many teachers. One of my favorite teachers is Vishen Lakhiani of Mindvalley. My first online business coach, Chanel - the publisher of this book - has us listen to Bob Proctor *every day* to help with our mindset. In the meditation, Proctor mentions Lakhiani. After researching Lakhiani, I realized what a phenomenal company he runs teaching some of the brightest minds, top performers, and contemporary thought leaders. He outlines the steps he uses to teach bending reality in a program that he has contributed to called the Silva Method. He mentions that there are four levels to personal growth and consciousness that exist on a continuum and that there are different tools to use at different levels

Vishen Lakhiani's 4 Levels of Consciousness

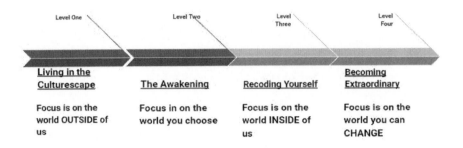

According to Lakhaini, the first state is level one, or the victim stage: *Living in the Culturescape*. Everything in the world around us is at fault or to blame for our lives. Personal growth is not high on the radar; people are simply existing or surviving. One may be overly religious or hooked on dogma and following the ideas of other humans. Life is very conventional and traditional. I spent the first twenty-five years of my life in stage one. I made mistake after mistake, bumbling through life trying to make everyone happy and succeeding at none of it. I had "successes" in the conventional sense of the word, for instance, university degrees, a stable career, a nice car, a family... but I was still merely existing. I had not healed much and didn't know how. I was searching for the meaning of life and wanted to know my purpose.

In the second stage, level two, we realize *The Awakening*. We realize that the world is NOT happening TO us. We realize we choose our experiences. We set goals and utilize the power of intention. Personal growth is important at this stage. Shifting our reality becomes within the realm of possibility; for example, we realize that we can bio-hack our bodies and decide how we age. Time is spent creating vision boards and using creative visualization. Affirmations are a powerful level two tool. The movie *The Secret'* was such a *powerful* influence on me at this stage, and it took me the better part of ten to twelve years to transition along the continuum from stage one to stage two. Others may transition in months. At times, I'd take two steps forward and then three steps back, it seems. I would seek out the healers, learn the history, join the movements, buy the books, do the fasts, get the colonics, take the supplements, go to the worship services, complete the journal prompts, etcetera and continue to look outward for answers that could only be found within.

In the third stage, people move beyond what Lakhaini referred to as the conventional modalities. Tools that are fantastic and produce amazing results at level two do not work as effectively. Level three is when we "recode" ourselves, where our thoughts are creating our reality, and where we are focused on the world inside of us. The outside world is still important, of course, but more time and energy are spent recalibrating and shaping our internal world. Meditation and altered states of consciousness are the tools of choice at this level. At this level, we are aware that we can be divinely guided through life, and we open ourselves up to it. We welcome that divine intervention and actively seek multiple ways to cultivate more time in altered states of consciousness.

LEVEL THREE WARNING: Prepare for a "Beautiful Destruction"

One of the *most* important takeaways has been the fact that as we start to inch along the continuum closer to level four and begin consistently incorporating level three tools and techniques; it may feel like our life explodes, implodes, or otherwise falls apart. He mentions that if you are not prepared, it is easy to feel as though one is absolutely being punished by the Universe. During his "beautiful destruction", Lakhaini had a major injury to his knee at forty-three years old, his childhood home caught fire with his parents in it (they survived). Also, his nineteen-year marriage ended, and he got divorced. Devastating, right? Well... all of it happened within six weeks. This was his "beautiful destruction".

Similarly, I had a series of tragic circumstances happen between 2018-2020. September 2, 2018, was the beginning of my "beautiful destruction". I talk at length about it in a chapter I authored in the book collaboration called *Birth (Volume II): Stories of Birth, Renewal, and Birthing a New Earth*, available on Amazon.com.

I remember being stuck *deep* in a depression, crying, and wondering, *"Why* is this happening TO me?" At one point, during my pregnancy, I was stuck in bed for three weeks straight, and my children ate oatmeal and fruit for breakfast, PB & J for lunch, and pizza, salad, and wings every night via Uber Eats because I absolutely couldn't muster the energy to get up and do anything. Unlike Lakhaini, no one had prepared me... so I didn't understand that all of this was happening FOR me. I was simultaneously in intensive outpatient counseling, group therapy, and family therapy. I had a coach or counselor for every part of my life, it seemed.

In a nutshell, I had a whirlwind courtship but abusive marriage involving infidelity. A pregnancy that I spent alone. I was clinically diagnosed with depression and anxiety because of that situation combined with job-related stress. I moved from my hometown of thirty years to escape and started over with my young children and infant. My family survived a devastating multi-vehicle, hit-and-run accident with an eighteen-wheeler in which all four of my children were injured - one severely. I started a new job and prepared for a new career while finishing up my second Master's degree. Then 2020 saw me start not one but *two* LLCs - one to help others who have survived trauma to rebuild their lives. Also in that year I filed and finalized my divorce and completed a Mental Health Peer Counselor training with the Georgia Mental Health Consumer Network. Additionally, I became a number one bestselling author, secured my first keynote speaker engagement, and invested in my first business coach.

I didn't understand that as we ascend to level four, the Universe comes in and will whisk away ANYTHING and EVERYTHING that is not serving our best interest. People, situations, possessions, relationships, finances…nothing is off-limits. This was part of my "beautiful destruction". And this disruption and reorganization is required for us to reach the next level up in our lives. It changes your life completely. And it is our job to mine the gold and the diamonds out of the rubble. It's our job to take the bricks thrown at us and use them to build the life we want. During this time, keep an attitude of gratitude. Learn the lessons and ascend to the next level!

At the fourth state of personal growth, people are the most fulfilled, feel the most expressed, and are absolutely, positively changing the world. Level four is simply MAGIC! And new levels require new tools. Believe it or not, conventional goal setting is not a level four tool. Neither is what we typically think of as intention. Divine guidance and divine intervention are at play. *Being* is an aspiration. We do not set our goals... a Higher Power over our lives or Source sets the goals. We are the vessel through which that power expresses and manifests those goals.

As such, a deep sense of connectedness among you and everything around you emerges. Human consciousness and unity are more important than socially constructed divisions. We heighten and tap into intuition constantly. We receive downloads from the Universe at this stage. Ideas and inspiration flow effortlessly. We can sit and write whole chapters of books or complete entire manuscripts in a setting. Creativity is abundant, and whatever our gifts are, they flow with ease. We understand the importance of inspired action and alignment.

People at level four are a "lucky" bunch whose lives are FULL of coincidences. 😄

Additionally, people at level four encounter seven more qualities that will be experienced consistently in this level. The qualities are bliss, immunity to overwhelm, relationships, inspiration on demand, abundance, flow, and ease. Using a technique that

Lakhiani calls *merging*, we rapidly accelerate the time between our dreams, our vision, and our reality.

Currently, I am knocking at the front door or level four. The door is ajar, and I can see inside. I know that it is absolutely fabulous on the other side, and I am so excited for the day that I look back and read this chapter to see just how far my quantum leap has taken me.

If any of this resonates and you feel compelled to reach different levels, the first step is to consider a compelling "why?" Why do you want to transform? What are you trying to uncover, or unlock? Answering this will give you clarity and help you stay the course when life seemingly goes haywire! My why is to create the legacy that I want to leave for my family.

Next, take inventory of how you see yourself. At which level are you today? Is that where you want to be? If not, what are you prepared to do to bend your reality and get to where you want to be? It helps to know what the tools are at every level and the order suggested in which we could use them.

The Tools for Bending Reality

Keep in mind, any process and tools that we use must absolutely align with our current level of consciousness. If you are a level one, do not try to skip to level four. Trust the process. Using the correct tools in the correct order will allow a person to continuously level up. Level four people are the visionaries who shift the culture and create their own culture. They create their own rules, make their own code, and influence many as they go.

Level One Tool

Lakhaini shares a level one tool called *segment intending*, that he learned from Esther Hicks. It is quick to use and based on imagining. If you would like to, try it when you first wake up and think of the day in terms of segments. If you've ever seen an elementary school teacher's schedule, then you have an idea of how to segment a day. If you use a planner, it is the same concept. Think about how the day is going to unfold in two- to three-hour segments from the time you wake up to the time you go to sleep. Divide your day into anywhere from four to ten segments.

For example:

Sample Segment

5-7 am	Wake, meditate and workout. Personal Growth.
7-8 am	Commute
8-11 pm	AM Meetings
11 am – 1 pm	Lunch
1-4 pm	Post Lunch Meetings
4-6 pm	Evening calls
6-7 pm	Commute
7-8 pm	Dinner and family time
8-10 pm	Relax and bedtime

As you think about each segment, begin to affirm statements such as, "I see myself having an AMAZING morning. Everything goes smoothly, my meditation is deep and meaningful. My workout builds and strengthens my body." Positively affirm and set an intention for what you want to happen for each segment of your day. Skeptics can think of it as a game of *Wouldn't It Be Nice If...?* Do this every day and see what happens! Additionally, listening to guided meditations is fabulous at this stage. Even more powerful? Create your own! The sound of our own voice helps when reprogramming our subconscious.

Level Two Tools

Powerful tools at level two are creative visualization and vision boards. In creative visualization, we enter an altered state and imagine exactly the life we want. Lakhaini prefers Jose Silva's Silva Method which activates different brain waves such as alpha waves. For at least three minutes daily, with the eyes raised at a fifteen-degree angle above the horizon, we practice visualizing exactly what we want our life to be like as though we are watching it on a television screen at least six feet right in front of you. Activate all senses by imagining what we see, hear, feel, touch, taste, and smell. The key is expectancy. You must come out of the session with a sense of expectancy. The feeling after you finish visualizing should have you like, "Yes, it's coming!" If you have doubts, visualize again. Each time doubt creeps in, visualize again until you have that feeling of expectancy.

Level Three Tool

At level three, when we are recoding ourselves, our intuition is the main tool. The guidance that we once sought from outside of ourselves is replaced with inner knowing and understanding. It will lead us in the direction of our highest self. When we are using our intuition correctly, our intentions become aligned with our deepest desires so that we manifest what we really want. When we set goals that come from our societal programming, culture, media and advertising, religion or any number of other external influences, we may manifest but what we create will not truly satisfy at the soul level. Our intuition guides our inspiration, which then becomes our goal. Our goal now is going to be fully aligned with our wants and needs. Activating and really listening to our deep inner voice is the goal of this lesson. Here is where accessing altered states of mind is critical. Moving from the beta state to the alpha and then the theta needs to be learned. Delta is a fourth state that can be accessed, although much of the bulk at level three happens in alpha and theta states.

Level Four Tool

Level four is when people become what Lakhaini refers to as extraordinary. It's where connection, intuition, intention, and divine guidance are working synergistically. The tool to make all of the magic happen: *merging*. Merging requires us to use the energy of the world around us. We live in an energetic universe; we experience a lot in the physical realm, but there is so much more in different domains. In level four, people are tuned more into energetic realms, use energy clearing and energy healing. Our intuition is clear, we can manifest much more quickly, and our creativity will increase. We will find ourselves more grounded and present in the moment, and we will have the courage to honor our purpose. We will be better able to use our minds to help heal ourselves. As a result of merging, we will become extremely self-aware, work from our strengths, and improve any challenge areas.

Over the past few years, I have enjoyed my journey of continual expansion and personal growth. I have been given tools that permit me to understand my life from a deeper, more spiritual perspective. I have widened my perspective and started tapping into the larger, cosmic, multiversal, timeless, energetic, and more collective experience of life. My life has improved in all areas as I've moved from level one, to two, to three. I was unprepared for my "beautiful destruction". Prayerfully, you, dear reader, will be more prepared the day yours comes.

I will continue to strengthen my ability to recreate my reality by keeping the faith, learning, showing up for myself, and taking inspired action. 2021 is the year I will merge! And so it is. It would be lovely to have you as part of my community as you witness the magic unfold. If this resonates, let's connect and keep in touch! Friend request, follow, and engage… and I'll do the same with you.

It's been an absolute pleasure and an honor to share this information with you. It's greatly impacted me along my journey, and I hope that there are at least a few nuggets of inspiration that you can take away and perhaps incorporate.

With love and gratitude,

Naomi Beverly
M.A., M.Ed.

About the Author

Naomi Beverly is a Transformational Coach, two-time No.1 Amazon International Bestselling Author, Mental Health Peer Support Specialist, and singer from the United States of America. Her company, Naomi Beverly Coaching LLC, helps people rebuild their lives after trauma one-on-one or in a supportive group community using self-publishing for self-care plus other tools and strategies. Her favorite types of books are those dealing with Social-Emotional Learning.

Naomi Beverly holds a B.A. in Broadcasting, Telecommunications, and Mass Media, an M.A. in Education, and an M.Ed. in Instructional Design.

During her free time, she enjoys dancing, yoga, meditation, working out, eating well, and being in nature. Naomi is the mother of four amazing children, two of whom have self-published and are in business for themselves. Their company is Sound Design and Development LLC.

Website: www.naomibeverlycoaching.com
Facebook: www.facebook.com/groups/selfpublishselfcare
Email: naomi@naomibeverlycoaching.com

Genetic Healing®: Live Your Best Possible Life!

By Bianca Glodt

Hello my dear readers,

Congratulations on taking the first step towards a more fulfilled, happy and healthy life by reading this book; that is amazing! It means you are searching for answers, thinking outside the box and open-minded towards new ways of living. These qualities are more necessary than ever in the times ahead of us.

You have a burning desire to connect with life on a deeper level, try out new, innovative, creative ways of living. Your intuition is whispering to you there has to be more out there than just the obvious, old fashioned ways of living, healing, doing and thinking. You want to live your best possible life whilst creating a bright and abundant future, not only for yourself but for all humanity.

Maybe you are reading this book because you have one specific area in your life you need help with. Maybe you are yearning for the breakthrough that will lead your life in an even better direction.

Maybe you are one of those people with an area in your life which effortlessly turns out great while other areas are completely resistant to progress despite all your efforts.

I'm curious... Have you read a ton of books looking for the 'magic' solution for your problem, have you asked friends or even asked Mr. Google countless times for advice? If you recognize yourself in this description, you are certainly not alone!

It can be frustrating to strive relentlessly to solve a problem that just won't budge, despite every new therapy, method or concept you try.

Would you believe me if I told you your problem probably didn't start with you; that its roots began a long time ago in a faraway place?

I invite you to join me on a fabulous journey into Genetic Healing®. Together we will transcend time and space, to the source of genetic imprints. You will learn how they shape our lives and how they can be transformed to achieve a more fulfilling and radiant life.

Nowadays, this concept of surpassing space and time is entirely plausible. There are many pioneers amongst scientists, philosophers and spiritual teachers who are writing and talking about this subject worldwide. In the world of biological science, involving complex data sequencing genomes and characterizing proteins, most developmental biologists accept there is a need for a more holistic or integrative model of human existence.

To begin, I will introduce you to the concepts of morphic energy and epigenetics, which form the foundation of the Genetic Healing® method.

Morphogenetic fields

From a very young age, my daughter has carried around a little plush octopus. She has always been fascinated by these animals. And so, became I. These animals are a perfect example to explain how living beings connect to the morphic field as a survival mechanism.

From the moment of birth, the tiny octopuses venture out into the water independently. They are born with complex survival skills of movement and self-camouflage; they have the ability to adapt their skin color and texture to their surroundings and grow horns on their heads. These remarkable creatures can 'walk', as if on two legs and precisely use geometry to locate the exact spot to drill mollusk shells for food, which requires tremendous intelligence.

It's extraordinary and somewhat mysterious how the octopus is born with all the innate skills it needs for survival, since the female dies as her eggs hatch and the male disappears after mating. Biologist Rupert Sheldrake suggested that such a phenomenon can be explained by morphogenetic fields.

Within a species, these fields contain data which have been transmitted from past generations through a frequency called morphic resonance. The fields relating to the control of the nervous system are inherited in the same way, thus transmitting a collective, instinctive memory to the next generation.

Morphogenetic fields can be influenced by every individual. Everyone both draws upon and contributes to the collective memory of the species, allowing the evolution of behavioral patterns. This is a much more efficient and fast way of learning than the traditional methods. An octopus can learn new skills and transmit them to other octopuses living in a different part of the ocean within a short period of time.

Animals inherit the successful habits of their species which becomes what is commonly described as instinct. Similarly, human societies have memories transmitted within different cultures, inheriting physical, emotional, mental and cultural habits.

It is incredible that, despite being great distances apart, individuals within social groups are still connected and communicating through these fields. Essentially, the aforementioned octopus is not alone in its solitary lifestyle, since it is connected to this higher intelligence as well as its fellow octopuses. Many species in the animal kingdom use telepathy to communicate. In our perception, telepathy is a paranormal phenomenon, but it is actually natural, not supernatural. Unbeknownst to many, it is also common amongst people, particularly those who know each other well.

Despite a continuous connection to the morphic field, we are not always consciously aware of it. Most people have already experienced morphic knowledge and energy. It can be described as the feeling of intuition, where we 'just felt' or 'just knew' that something was going to happen, or we instinctively knew what to do in a fragment of a second.

Creating a stronger connection with and awareness of the 'knowing field' is an ability every human naturally possesses. It can be trained like a muscle, allowing us to differentiate between personal feelings, beliefs and the information received from this collective energy field.

An accessible sort of collective memory, along with information from past generations, is transmitted to each of us by 'epigenetic tags'.

Epigenetics

Epigenetics is a relatively new area of study exploring how different factors influence gene activity.

The decryption of the human DNA code in 2001 was a huge scientific breakthrough. Many people believed this advance in knowledge could change everything. Indeed, the researchers pushed open the door, but it was dark behind it. The 23,000 human genes that have been deciphered proved insufficient in explaining human biology and functioning in its entirety. It turns out that DNA is only basic equipment of the body.

The human body contains around two hundred different cell types. Although all of them initially have the same genetic make-up, the cells themselves vary greatly, for example, heart and liver cells are very different. Researchers have discovered that each cell type activates different genes on the DNA strand by binding special proteins to it. Each cell in the body only uses the genes necessary for its function.

This discovery that genes can essentially be 'switched on and off' gave the impetus for a branch of research that is booming today: epigenetics.

Epigenetic tags are molecular chains that contain additional data and are attached to the DNA. With this information, the cell ultimately decides how to control the genes and it does so under many, many influences.

The study of bees, for example, shows how environmental influences can affect the regulation of the gene switches. All the female bees in a hive, the queen and the worker bees, have exactly the same genetic make-up.

The worker bees are physically small and collect and feed the pollen. The queen grows to a significantly larger size, lives longer, never flies to a flower and only reproduces.

How can such different beings arise from the same genetic make-up? All bees share the exact same DNA, but because they develop under different environmental influences, they turn into different organisms. It is the bees' nutrition that makes the difference. Queen larvae are fed exclusively with royal jelly while worker bees receive the precious substance only for a short time. This small divergence is enough for two different organisms to arise from the same genetic material.

Nutritional input has very similar effects on the human body. Food is only one of several relevant factors in epigenetic switches. Due to environmental influences, molecules can penetrate the cell nucleus, which can lead to a change in the switches on the genetic material. During normal cell division, the DNA thread is chemically read and copied. However, in the event that foreign molecules attach to the DNA, the reading will be disturbed. Thus, it will be copied incorrectly, increasing the potential for illnesses or mental disorders to arise. This change, resulting from environmental influences, can be passed on to subsequent generations.

Of course, it's not all bad news, since positive events also establish themselves as imprints in the same way.

It is a purely chemical process that takes place in each of our body's cells. Molecular chains wrap around the genes, enabling their information to be deciphered. These molecular chains known as energetic tags are present at birth; the genes we inherit from our parents are passed on through cell division, and we already possess activated and deactivated genes. In each of our 60-100 trillion body cells, our DNA string is rolled up containing over 23,000 genes and many more energetic tags, where the information passed on from our ancestors that ultimately shapes us, is stored.

Post-traumatic stress disorder, for example, not only affects an individual's genes but also those of future generations. The release of cortisol, for example, prompts the cell to activate or deactivate various genes which 'remember' this trauma as an epigenetic imprint. Subsequent generations often suffer from the same diseases and anxiety disorders, since the responsible gene switches remain activated or deactivated.

Since we are the result of our genes and the epigenetic variation in our genes, as well as being conditioned by external influences, we have a certain responsibility towards our descendants' futures as well as our own.

In summary, one can say that genes shape us but at the same time we shape our genes.

What is Genetic Healing®?

Upon first learning about Genetic Healing®, I was amazed at the variety of unimaginable healing possibilities that could be explored using this method. It represents a whole new dimension of healing, from which growth and insight can emerge. I had no idea how much this method would change my life and the lives of others for the better.

Genetic Healing®, in simple terms, is the energetic removal of epigenetic imprints in the genes. It was invented and developed by Mrs. Gabriele Petrig, who is an experienced psychotherapist, personal development coach, and an expert in Systemic Constellation Work (an alternative therapeutic method) since 1995. During her work with children and adults, she became more and more aware of the fact that a great deal of problems are caused by a complex entanglement of events. Determined to understand the root causes of her clients' problems, she developed the Systemic Constellation Work further. In 2016, she presented this new idea to the world, developing the Genetic Healing® method in collaboration with her sister, Mrs. Monika Klotz.

Genetic Healing® is a unique energetic healing method; it is an extension of the Systemic Constellation Work, and its effects reach the cellular level. This method functions at a high energetic frequency and allows significant expansion of our consciousness, enabling the deactivation of traumatic experiences, illnesses, behavioral patterns, belief systems, and familial imprints that have been epigenetically inherited.

About eight months ago, a client came to me with a problem. She had been overweight since her teenage years and had been eating compulsively. She always felt like she had not eaten enough. We discovered her genetic imprints were programmed by the circumstances of an ancestor; unable to access food, they had died of starvation during a war. Her body responded to this tragic 'memory' by accumulating fat and guiding her to eat more as a means of protection against famine. A month after working with her, she had started a new diet and lost thirty-five pounds. Her story illustrates how the living conditions of our ancestors can unconsciously impact our behavioral patterns.

Recent scientific studies show that we are shaped +/- 10% by our DNA and +/- 90% by our epigenetic imprints. Not only are we the result of our mother's and father's genes, but the experiences of our ancestors significantly impact our lives more than previously assumed. Genetic Healing® aims to alter these energetic tags with ways to deactivate or activate these molecular chains and the information they contain. There are around four million of these 'switches' on our DNA, but only a very small percentage are active. A great deal of potential lies dormant in our DNA, waiting to be activated.

It is common knowledge that traumatic experiences have effects on our physical, mental, and emotional well-being, but it is lesser known how the experiences from our ancestors can recur in our bodies and still provoke a reaction today.

Victims' and perpetrators' traumas are passed on, and can still be felt by their descendants, although they have not experienced it themselves, it still affects them. For example, a person can constantly feel guilty, despite having done nothing to cause it. Others may have severe anxieties or trust issues without understanding where they come from.

Most mental and physical health issues have their root cause in past traumatic experiences. Trauma activates and deactivates specific genes that can result in illness, unhealthy behavioral patterns, or belief systems that do not serve us.

A Genetic Healing® session

In a Genetic Healing® session, the practitioner identifies the original issue through a very deep energetic connection with the client, finding out where the client's problem originated. It sometimes goes back ten to fifteen generations to discover a tragedy in the family that is affecting the client's life. It is not uncommon for family structures to continue to manifest several generations later.

The experiences leading to certain problems vary from person to person, but the root causes are always very specific. One client, for example, had a phobia of mice and rats. Just looking at these vermin made her feel nauseous. In a session it turned out that a female ancestor had been raped five generations prior. When I asked her which feature of the rodent made her feel so scared and disgusted, she replied, 'the tail'. Even though she couldn't remember exactly what happened to one of her ancestors, she still carried the memory of this event as anxiety in her body and mind.

Immediately after the Genetic Healing® session, she no longer related to her fear; it had become incomprehensible to her how she could be afraid of a harmless mouse.

A Genetic Healing® session transforms the original event that caused this epigenetic imprint and brings it into healing. Whilst this may have happened to an ancestor, it could also be caused by an event in the client's present life.

This was the case with a client in his forties who came to me because of his psoriasis. In the past he had tried many ointment therapies and support groups, but nothing brought him long-term relief. During the Genetic Healing® session we discovered the root cause of his skin issues. When he was ten-years-old, he was beaten and bullied by classmates on the way home from school. This event released so much stress hormones in his body, that its effects reached down to the cellular level and activated the genes causing the illness. Since that moment the psoriasis kept other people at a 'safe' distance and him 'potentially' safe. After the energetic deactivation of the relevant 'gene switches' it took eight weeks until he was psoriasis free.

When the practitioner is in contact with the topic at the root cause, he or she works with the Genetic Healing® energy which operates beyond space and time. With this energy, the trauma is transformed and the gene switches are permanently switched off. Most of the time, the change becomes noticeable for the client whilst the new matrix is flowing into their body cells which are being 'informed' of the new information. During this transformation process, the clients feel something is happening, often reporting, "I don't know what you did but I feel lighter, it's like a weight has been lifted."

When the 'switches' have been changed, the problem that has been treated is often no longer understandable for the client. It seems unimportant, and the client feels a sense of detachment from it.

With all the sessions of Genetic Healing® I have done, every client felt an improvement after the session. Some completely changed from one moment to the next. Sometimes they couldn't remember the problem they had. Their facial expression changes, they report feeling peaceful, and there is a sparkle in their eyes. For others, it may take several weeks to see the effects, but every client I've worked with has noticed major changes in their life.

Since we humans are accustomed to different behaviors and structures, we have to learn to live with the transformed epigenetic imprints. There are meditations that can help the client to focus on the new structures and come into alignment with them. Genetic Healing® also offers ways to help people align with their goals and the new structures that were created during the session.

A Genetic Healing® session is extremely liberating; many worries, problems and life dramas can just dissolve and heal. I'm extremely grateful to practice Genetic Healing® and am blessed to have other practitioners around me, so that I can receive healings myself.

Throughout the last year, I have experienced the benefits of Genetic Healing® first-hand. I have transformed many belief systems that have existed in my family for generations into ones that actually help me thrive and create my own identity. I have gained new insight into why I have stayed in unhealthy relationships for so long in the past, allowing me to finally break free from these patterns. These are just a few of many examples. Overall, Genetic Healing® has been a real blessing in my life, leaving me feeling much more grounded and peaceful as a person.

There are many new healing modalities around the globe nowadays, allowing people to choose the right one for them, with the method or concept they identify with the most. At heart, we all have the capacity to heal ourselves and nurture others. Spirit, energy, thought, intention, skillful practice, and belief are universal and available to all people. Yet, as we are all unique and individual expressions of life force, we all need different ways to achieve healing.

Currently, the consciousness of mankind is preparing itself for huge leaps and discoveries. By supporting the universal healing power every human naturally possesses, Genetic Healing® can facilitate these developments and innovations through helping us live happier, more harmonious and loving lives.

The magnificence of Genetic Healing® is that it can be applied in a very simplistic way; it works for a wide range of problems, and the effects are very powerful. I haven't seen any other kind of method or energy that allows one to connect with the healing source on such a deep level, nor with such timely results. Furthermore, it deepens our relationship with our ancestors, with others, and our own deep importance and vulnerability when we realize we are all ONE.

If you are looking for more information on Genetic Healing®, want to book an individual session or are interested in learning the Genetic Healing® technique yourself, you can find more information on our websites or simply search for our names and Genetic Healing® in a search engine. Sessions can be held in person as well as online.

It is the desire of Mrs. Gabriele Petrig and all Genetic Healing® practitioners that all humans achieve freedom from their epigenetic imprints of the past so that they can live their best possible life and create a better future for humanity. Every healed trauma is yet another one that will not be passed on to our descendants. Our genetic makeup and the associated imprints are no longer our fate; we hold a huge potential in our hands to give our heritage and destiny a positive direction.

So, what can you do best to create a better life for yourself and humanity?

From an epigenetic point of view:

BE HAPPY, BE KIND AND LIVE YOUR BEST POSSIBLE LIFE!

About the Author

Bianca Glodt is a Genetic Healing® practitioner. Over the past twenty years, she has graduated and worked as a nurse, elementary teacher and wellness therapist. Over the course of her years of working with patients, students and clients, she has become increasingly aware of the complexity of human health and its dependence on environmental and epigenetic mechanisms.

Today, she uses her Genetic Healing® skills to help people overcome trauma and health issues through the transformation of their epigenetic imprint, enabling them to finally break free of past experiences and create their best possible life.

Website: www.beyondwellnesswithbianca.com
www.petrig-genetic-healing.de
Facebook Page: www.facebook.com/BeyondWellnesswithBianca
Facebook Group:
www.facebook.com/groups/beyondwellnesswithbianca
Email: zafalia@gmail.com

Pain Is Part of Your Purpose

By Kandis Troutman

"I don't dance in my underwear anymore."
~ Callie, Grey's Anatomy, Season 10

It's human nature to move, shift, or change for two reasons: pleasure or pain. Unfortunately, the majority of us choose the latter because society has trained us to believe that pleasurable decision making is selfish. The good news is that pain is part of our purpose and the trick is to understand how to use it as a tool of improvement, instead of allowing pain to become a cesspool of bitterness and resentment.

I was sitting on the sofa watching reruns of the Shonda Rhimes television sensation, *Grey's Anatomy*, when I heard the quote above and busted out crying. These were not what I call lady tears, you know silent, sweet, and polite. These were an ugly, snotty, messy, and can't catch my breath type of tears. Regardless of how they appeared on the surface, these were not sad tears. These were celebratory, joyful, praise the Lord, and Holy hallelujah tears! These were the tears I had held hostage for over ten years. The tears that were suppressed because releasing them earlier in my life might have led to a nervous breakdown. Tears that were hidden from family, friends, and especially my kid. These were the never let them see you sweat tears. I'm going to cry in my car as soon as you get out of my face tears. Now that I think about it, I should probably stop describing it as crying, because what happened at that moment was...I WEPT!

But remember I said, these were tears of joy. So why was I crying so hard over such a simple statement? Because Shonda Rhimes summed up what I couldn't put into words. Let me give you an important characteristic about me, I'm a classically trained former dancer. This means I incorporate dance into everything I do. I dance when I cook, I dance when I create, I dance while I clean my house. I'm dancing right now as I write this chapter. Dance is my first love and my foundation. Dance is not just something I do, it is who I am. It has given me discipline, dedication, passion, innovation, and an escape strategy. I don't need a studio or a stage. I'm the most comfortable and authentic in my home, blinds open, candles lit, headphones on blast, and dancing in my underwear.

Now imagine me without dance in my life. Imagine me no longer listening or feeling inspired by music. Once upon a time, I was a woman so lost and numb, that I was simply a shell of my former self. I was existing because I had forgotten how to live. People who know me best consider me a free spirit, go all in, take-the-leap kind of woman and somehow, I had become someone who lacked fire.

I was a woman who had buried her feelings so deeply that instead of dancing, pretending became my default setting.

Perhaps you've heard the phrase, "Every woman has a breaking point". This is not just a phrase, it's a phase. Most people believe it refers to when a woman decides to leave a toxic relationship. However, it is so much deeper than that. The phrase is a description of what happens when a woman recognizes her potential, sees herself through God's eyes, decides to break her limiting beliefs, and commits to releasing her potential. The *breaking point* is not about breaking away from a relationship. The breaking point is the process of freeing yourself from bondage in the mind, releasing fear, being comfortable with vulnerability, activating your voice, and trusting your intuition enough to take action. The breaking point is not a singular moment, it's a movement. It's the process of transformation required to break glass ceilings and step directly into your divine destiny. You are usually unaware of your breaking point season. It's one of those lessons that can only be understood after you go through the experience. Honestly, you don't even know what your breaking point is until a moment, incident or experience causes something to fall off the shelf inside your soul and break you wide open.

Miserable doesn't even begin to describe my mental, physical, and spiritual state. Literally, at my breaking point, I dropped to my knees and began praying. I prayed daily, hourly, heck I'm sure it was every minute some days. I wasn't asking for more money, a better job, or even a new car. All I wanted was for God to give me a way out of my marriage. My prayers weren't composed of beautiful lyrics. These were begging, grieving, deep despair types of prayers. One prayer, in particular, I will never forget because it was the rawest, hence why God answered it. Beside my bed and on my knees, I yelled out, "God, I don't care if it's messy, embarrassing, or costly, just please just get me out!" Spoiler alert, the prayer was answered, and it was messy, embarrassing, costly, as well as the best thing that ever happened to me. However, if you know anything about God, the answer to my prayer didn't look like what I was expecting. My out, my escape route, my greatest opportunity came when I peed on a stick.

Yep, I'm talking about a pregnancy test. The moment two little lines formed on not one but three different tests, I realized that the way I was living was no longer an option because I was having a kid. And what God knew that I had yet to discover, was what I couldn't figure out how to do for myself, I would figure out for my kid. And if you know like I know, a mother that is in protection mode is a powerful being. In other words, my motherly instincts kicked in and I was ready to dance in my undies again! And dance I would! But first remember I had to go through the messy, embarrassing, and costly that I mentioned previously. So now let me explain how I got here.

Mistake #1: I decided to plan a wedding within a year of my father's death. I lacked the wisdom that you should not make any life-changing decisions within a year of losing a loved one.

Mistake #2: I honestly never wanted to be married. I lacked the wisdom and courage to be exactly who I am designed to be instead of trying to fit in with society's standards.

Mistake #3: I did not like or love my ex exactly the way he was. I lacked the wisdom that I cannot fix anyone but myself and people have to want to change.

I knew my wedding was a mistake. In my soul, I knew this was temporary. Due to the fact that I couldn't articulate what or why, besides my gut, I completed the process. I know what you are thinking; "Why did you go through with the ceremony?" Honestly, because I start what I finish. This characteristic showed up as a flaw because I was out of balance. Later, it would become one of my greatest assets because instead of quitting when things began to collapse around me, I just kept going. To be fair, my ex didn't want to be there either. While I entered my vows with a ridiculous amount of doubt, he entered his vows with a girlfriend. And thus, began the messy, embarrassing, and costly, that would lead me down the path of purpose.

Women have the beautiful gift of intuitiveness. Our intuitiveness is here to guide, warn, and protect us from danger in the future. It's a personal bubble of protection. Only when we are willing to listen, trust, and take heed can our intuition serve its purpose. This means, women can sense things before they happen. We feel it in our spirit, it shows up in our bodies, and it's just *knowing* that something is not right. Now the problem is that most women have been trained to ignore and/or, even worse, not trust their intuition.

And where did this horrible training originate? Well, I believe that some man whose woman was calling him out on his crap immediately reacted with, "You're crazy", and that man taught every other man how to use this phrase to make women second-guess themselves, ignore their intuition hence diminishing our gift.

My mother used to tell me that when I was full, I would push away from the table. In other words, when you are fed up with taking crap, you will seek an out. My body was physically changing which meant my mind and spirit had to shift to stay in alignment with my new assignment of becoming a mother. I was aware of what I ate, listened to, how I walked, my finances, and my environment. In other words, I was becoming present. And the more present I became, the more "full" I felt, the more I was pushing away from the "table" that was my marriage. I was hyper-aware of my thoughts and feelings because I knew my son would have the same experience. And that's when the magic happened, I slowly started hearing and more importantly TRUSTING my intuition again. My intuition used to be calm, polite and whispered. Now she was bold, blunt, and demanding. I was slowly coming out of my unconscious coma. What I didn't know was that my intuition was preparing me for what was to come. The answers to my prayers were on the way. To recognize them as a blessing, I would have to be open, willing, and ready to shift my perspective, or else I would miss the opportunity. Being aware of what I ate not only helped develop a healthy baby but ensured I would be physically prepared for single motherhood. Being aware of my thoughts, helped shift my perspective from focusing on the problem to defining the solution. I was now intentional, so instead of using my discernment to hunt down my ex's indiscretions, I was organizing and nesting. I sat down and created a step-by-step plan. It included hiring an attorney, negotiating my rent, reworking my budget, and interviewing nannies. Simultaneously as I grew a tiny human, I was also developing as a woman. And for the first time, my ex's narcissistic personality helped my situation. While I was busy plotting, planning, shifting, and growing, he remained completely self-centered and oblivious to the changes happening all around him. Hence, giving me the time and space to lay the foundation for a smooth exit.

My ex's relationship with his girlfriend showed up the first time like a molehill; I tried to forgive and move forward because that's what a "good wife" should do right? She made her next appearance as a volcano and I threw the good wife theory out the window and chose to be "bad all by myself" instead. The eruption began as a rumble and quickly grew to a massive explosion. It started with my ex saying, "I'm going bowling." My simple response, "I have a bad feeling and think you should stay home." And without hesitation, his immediate reaction, "YOU'RE CRAZY", and he left. I had no insight into why I felt what I did. It wasn't that I wanted him at the house with me. It wasn't that I was blind to who he would be with because that no longer mattered to me. I thought it could have been a warning about a car wreck, or something terrible happening at the location. My only responsibility was to trust my intuition, say what I felt, and take action, which was to tell him. What I didn't know was that the girlfriend was done sitting on the sidelines and she was going to let the entire world know.

At a crazy hour, my intuition woke me up and said check Twitter. My stomach was in knots and my anxiety was on ten, but again I trusted and took action. With one tweet, the girlfriend released me. As I read it, my initial response was THANK YOU. I called my best friend, apologized for the hour, and told her what had happened and that I would begin the divorce process in the morning. She asked what I was going to do right now, and without hesitation, I said, "REST". I hung up, and I slept. I slept like a woman who had not slept in a decade because I hadn't. I slept like a woman that was no longer living a nightmare. I didn't just sleep, I RESTED. My mind and body could rest because my spirit finally had what it had been craving: peace. It was done. No more questioning and tolerating lies. No more mind tricks and manipulation tactics. No more being the lead planner for pity parties. No more pretending I was happy at his family functions. No more making excuses for his constant failures. No more carrying the burden for someone else's brokenness and dysfunction.

The girlfriend assumed she and I were in the same boat, that we wanted the same thing, my ex. What she didn't realize was that I wanted to raise my son in a happy and loving environment, which my ex could never provide. A single tweet that was designed to shame and humiliate me came in the form of a gift from someone who considered herself my enemy.

Seven months pregnant and it was time to make some grown-up

decisions. I was either going to become a victim of my circumstances, a statistic, or I was going to transform the obstacles into opportunities. With all that was happening, my main priority was to deliver a healthy baby. Although my prayer was answered, that didn't mean my ex and especially the girlfriend were going to make it an easy transition. Therefore, keeping my emotions in check, staying focused, and activating my optimism was imperative. After the "tweet of freedom", I awoke the next morning and called into work because I was putting pleasure first. I opened all the blinds, lit some candles, threw on some music, and all of a sudden, I found myself crying but even better...DANCING! I was dancing again. I could hear and feel music again. I was creating steps again. I felt inspired and ALIVE again! I danced all day, even while I watched my ex drive past the house to see if my car was outside, and then drive away. I danced as I called my mother and his parents and let them know what had happened. I danced as I made an appointment with an attorney, made a list of my divorce requirements, combed through my finances, and changed passwords. The tasks that I could not seem to do for years, no longer felt overwhelming and scary, they felt appropriate, timely, and easy because I was finally in alignment.

The shenanigans from my ex and his girlfriend would continue for over a year. Sadly, I was a willing participant for the first three months, because my broken pieces were seeking a win. Yet, my spirit, my intuition, and my motherly instincts were pulling me in a different direction. The moment I stopped fighting with them is the moment the real work began. What they did or did not do was no longer my problem. And with that one decision, I committed myself to building the life I envisioned. It wasn't full of confusion and chaos, it was a life of inspiration, boldness, and creativity. It was a life that refused to accept pain over pleasure. It was a life that knew it was time for a gut-wrenching self-check.

Blaming my ex would have been the easy and cowardly method. I desired the tenacious and transformative strategy. So, I went the opposite direction and began questioning. How did I get here? How did I allow myself to be treated so poorly? Why would I tolerate someone who wasn't worthy of my time and energy? When did I become someone I didn't respect? Where did I lose my voice? How did a "good wife" equal no standards? When exactly did my dreams get deferred? How did I get so spiritually empty? Why was my life so off-course? When and how did pretending become my default setting? Why did I care what other people thought of me? When did I become comfortable living a lie? What was the purpose of this experience? And the hardest question, what do I want moving forward? I journaled to answer the questions because our own words reveal our deepest desires, insecurities, trauma, passions, and our truth.

I experienced a crazy amount of pain in the relationship with my ex and I have absolutely no regrets. Because the pain that felt unbearable at the time didn't destroy me; instead I allowed it to build me. It made me resilient. It made me courageous. It made me faithful. It made me confident. It made me relatable as well as impactful. It made me spiritually conscious and aware of my words and actions. It made me intentional and a woman composed of grace and mercy. It made me PURPOSEFUL. That pain didn't come to kill me, it came to teach me. It didn't come to humiliate me, it came to humble me. It didn't come to destroy my hopes and dreams, it came to remind me of the power that dwells within me. Without that experience, without that pain, I would have never hit my breaking point, and I would have missed my divine calling.

We are not designed to settle or simply exist. We are designed and destined for a unique purpose that is directly connected to how we are to be of service. However, uncovering and understanding your purpose will require you to experience pain. Like it or not, pain is part of the process. Pain has a way of pushing us out of our comfort zones, waking up our unconscious souls, and igniting our internal power. If you are open, pain can be one of your greatest resources. It is a springboard for transforming your potential into reality. Because pain is not just about you, it's to help you heal someone else.

Everybody and their mama promote that the path to happiness is to follow your "bliss". I don't subscribe to this singular teaching because number one, happiness is a temporary feeling which means it comes and goes like the wind, therefore, wisdom understands the importance of seeking and being rooted in JOY because it dwells inside the soul; number two let's not forget "bliss" is also for the ignorant. So, seek your purpose, which is the combination of your passions and pain. Your passions are the things that set your heart on fire and will keep you inspired. While your pain is directly connected to the experiences that you have overcome, therefore making you qualified to create and teach someone else the solution, otherwise known as being of service.

My experience with my ex led me to my purpose, eventually becoming my business. That business would become a tool to teach other women how to activate and trust their intuition, understand their purpose, and transform it into a prosperous business. So, when Callie stated, "I don't dance in my underwear anymore," my heart rejoiced because I realized I was no longer that woman!

About the Author

Kandis Troutman, MA is a creative thinker and communicator with corporate insight. She completed her undergraduate degree at Howard University before pursuing her Master's in Talent Development at Tusculum University. She teaches women how to transition their mindset from fear to faith, exchange confusion for clarity, and transform their purpose into prosperity. Her vision is to demonstrate the possibilities when you know, understand, and trust your intuition.

Known to her friends and clients as *The Tinkerbell Strategist* because she is gifted at transforming potential into paths of purpose. Kandis enjoys encouraging women to take action, laugh out loud, pursue freedom, and walk confidently into their destiny. She accomplishes this through her Purpose and Prosperity coaching and course programs. When she's not creating, she can be found hanging out with her son, reading yet another book, or traveling.

Website: www.thecreativearchitect.com
Facebook: www.facebook.com/TheCreativeArchitect
www.facebook.com/groups/PurposefulandProsperousWomen
Email: Solutions@TheCreativeArchitect.com

Adventures in Vulnerability: Openness in the Face of Catastrophe

By lavasjah shabre'
luh/vey/jh

"I think; therefore I am." - Rene Descartes, 1637
"I feel; therefore I am." - lavasjah shabre', 2020

We are all familiar with philosopher, Rene Descartes' famous philosophical statement, "I think; therefore I am." The idea is that the only certainty is this very statement - your capacity to think confirms your existence. In a spiritual sense, "I am" is all that is needed to confirm the beingness and divinity of life. From the Bible's "I am that I am" in Exodus to Hinduism's "Tattvamasi" which translates to "I am that" or "thou art that," the beingness or consciousness of existence gives life to living and meaning to life. Indian mystic and yogi, Sadhguru, says, "You are; therefore, you may think." I am a firm believer in this truth, yet year 2020 revealed layers of life somehow unbeknownst to me due to a direct, intense, conscious engagement with vulnerability.

The intensity and gravity of this past year propelled me into foreign territories literally, emotionally, mentally, spiritually and physically, as I am sure was the case for most if not everyone. 2020 seemed to be a spectacle, almost a theatrical display - a drama, horror, thriller and comedy all in one. We all collectively watched, experienced and participated in a whirlwind of a year - locally, nationally and globally. And although it was and is indeed a pandemic, each individual was personally affected, independent of the mutual, collective experience.

Personally, I chose to focus on how the experience of 2020 affected me emotionally as that is where the varied layers of existence revealed themselves the most. Emotions I'd never encountered jolted me into unfamiliar spheres of life where vulnerability became the cornerstone. This emphasis led me to the affirmation - "I feel; therefore I am."

Although I could not control the happenings in the world - politics, racism, bigotry, health crisis, global closures and overall suffering - and how they impacted my life on a macro scale, I figured I could try to use this experience on a micro level as a tool for deeper introspection, inner awareness and understanding. I could feel my feelings fully. I could sit with them wholly. I could allow myself to go through the motions instead of trying to control them, which I'm sure we are all guilty of doing.

As an advocate for productivity and self-care, I figured this would be the best option. What's more productive and nurturing than observing what's happening around you and how it makes you feel, recognizing its impact and then using those observations and recognitions for greater understanding, evolution and development. This seemed to be the only option.

What I noticed was the world's and my own immense vulnerability. I noticed the pervasiveness and expansiveness of vulnerability around me and the world at large and I decided to focus on it. Interestingly, I started 2020 with the intention to surrender to life, "to go with the flow"—a big deal for a recovering semi "control freak." I decided to simply book a one-way flight to India to study yoga and meditation and globetrot thereafter.

The flow was beautiful, at first; however, I could have never imagined what would unfold. In hindsight, 2020 was a continuous, arduous, audacious practice of vulnerability. I felt things I've never felt because I allowed myself to. I had no choice but to surrender to the happenings around me. And although "going with the flow" was my intention, when put to action, it seemed to just be a cliché that I was not ready to embody. Nevertheless, because I was forced to surrender, I was able to experience life in a remarkable way.

Although it shouldn't take a pandemic to push us to be open and fully experience the range of human emotion, the widespread vulnerability it caused somehow empowered me to go on this adventure of vulnerability consciously and intentionally. During the journey, there were many ups and downs, twists and turns, and here, I will share bits of the process with the hope that others can learn from my adventure of vulnerability. I hope it will inspire a more vulnerable, open world. I hope that it will help others become comfortable in the discomfort of uncertainty. I hope that it will encourage others to feel fully and honor their feelings, even the uncomfortable ones. I hope that it will inspire more intuitive, expansive, authentic living.

Vulnerability: the quality or state of being exposed to the possibility of being attacked or harmed, either physically or emotionally.

"The universe is made up of experiences that are designed to burn out your attachment, your clinging to pleasure, to pain, to fear, to all of it. And as long as there is a place where you're vulnerable, the universe will find a way to confront you with it." - Ram Dass

In the beginning, there were overwhelming feelings of excitement, gratitude, bliss, and curiosity. Everything seemed to be in flow as I ventured to the birthplace of yoga: India. Adventure, meditation, yoga, nature, spirituality, connection, friendship, zen. And then, an unprecedented, unexpected pandemic - an emotional rollercoaster - fear, worry, anxiety, doubt, vulnerability...

Reality is crashing down on me
The weight is hard to bear
The full immensity of reality is exerting pressure on my core
Not my mind, heart, body - my core
Breathe
Breathe through it

It's nice to feel sometimes
There's a certain aliveness in feeling
And sitting with the feeling
Despite the discomfort it brings
Triggered, restless, anxious, longing
Long gone

It's hard to process your emotions when you are so busy feeling them.

You don't want to cover up your emotions, drown them, sedate them away, you want to experience them. You want to feel them, process them and work through them.

They are just emotions, short-lived, ephemeral, coming and going, yet so heavy and intense. Why do they feel so heavy and intense? Maybe these are feelings you haven't felt before. Maybe these are feelings you haven't opened yourself to experience; the uncomfortable, uncertain, unknown. These require a certain level of openness and vulnerability, but are you willing to go there?

There's so much resistance to your surrender. A feeling arises and you shift your attention. At times, you may use your rational mind to process, but you seem to stop at a certain point each and every time - rationalization and compartmentalization.

This rationalization and compartmentalization is based on your past. How else will you make sense of your experience? You use your frame of reference which is solely based on what you know. What if you are experiencing something you've never experienced before? Using that previous frame of reference may not be useful for the processing of your present experience. It may even hinder your understanding of what's happening. You can be blinded by your past.

Of course, it's natural for human beings to create narratives to make sense of reality. It is in our DNA. It is the simplest option when faced with the influx of sensory, situational, and interpersonal information we process moment by moment. However, when processing an unfamiliar story, these narratives sometimes aren't compatible. With vulnerability, they usually aren't.

When feeling stuck in a foreign country, based on previous narratives, you might just simply book a flight elsewhere. On the other hand, in the unfamiliar times of a pandemic, this option is simply impossible.

When feeling stuck in a foreign country, based on previous narratives, you might just simply book a flight elsewhere or return "home". On the other hand, in the unfamiliar times of a pandemic, this option is simply impossible.

If you are living in a space with exasperating company, based on previous narratives, you might lash out or move away. On the other hand, in the unfamiliar times of a pandemic, these options would either be counterproductive or impossible.

What do you do? How do you process these emotions? How do you move past your discomfiture, unease, or vexation in these vulnerable situations?

Using your personal frame of reference based on your past experiences, habits, desires, baggage, and so on could lead you down a spiral. It could cause you to resist the experience, taint it, make an enemy out of it. Focusing on the patterns that align with your frame of reference could close you off from the experience entirely. It could prevent you from a profound encounter with the fullness of life, regardless of how disagreeable the experience is to your equilibrium, or what some could label: your ego.

In these situations of discomfort and uncertainty, you want to change the trajectory or remove yourself, escape. This is the rational response. Why not? You feel an uncomfortable emotion and you want to move on to something more pleasant. Why would you stay in the distress? Why torture yourself?

When these aren't options, your vulnerability comes alive. It becomes difficult to sit openly with your emotions without any apparent solution or action. To think something as natural as feeling could be so difficult. Why can't you just feel your feelings and let them go?

You wonder - is it safe to feel these emotions fully? Can I open myself up to this moment wholly? Do I lean into this moment of vulnerability? Am I even capable?

Then comes fear. You've had to be strong for so long; being vulnerable, unsure or what some might call "weak" scares you. The fear coerces you to maybe revert back to what you've always known: your reflexes - flight or fight, aggression, escapism, rationalization. First, you lose control of your feelings, then you lose control of your mind searching for a way back to your equilibrium. And it becomes a cycle.

I understand. You are simply protective of yourself, hence your defense mechanisms and resistance. But what are you protecting yourself from? What are you holding yourself back from?

If you are unable to adjust your life conditions to your liking or control them, what options do you have? Resist, fight, escape, dwell or suffer? Surrender seems to be the only acceptable option, and your defense mechanisms serve no purpose in surrender.

Surrender: to abandon oneself entirely to (a powerful emotion or influence); give in to.

With nothing else to do and nowhere else to turn, you surrender. You give in to the experience. You open your mind to observe the feeling, the situation, the condition. You analyze and dissect as a natural inclination and then you simply open your heart to accept the experience and your interpretation of it. With this encompassing awareness, you realize this is a learning moment, a teaching moment.

Living in this awareness instead of the clouds of your mind allows for a grander experience, a grander life even. You begin to cultivate a 360 view of what's happening around and within you. You question:

Is this feeling the end of the world? Is this situation the end of the world? What is the source of these tensions that make themselves evident in these moments of vulnerability? Trauma? Childhood? Ancestral? Is this just the way you are? Are you still trying to balance out all that you have experienced in your subconscious? Are you still dealing in the past unknowingly?

You learn. You understand. You *innerstand*. You grow. You soften around your edges to reach your core. You peel back the layers consciously. You cultivate compassion for yourself and your experience.

Compassion is something we've been taught to cultivate for external use. We often neglect to direct this compassion toward ourselves. This is the moment. Be gentle with yourself as you process your emotions and your circumstances. It isn't easy and it isn't painless. Pain is involved, but maybe they are growing pains and for those, you are thankful. You affirm:

I feel the pain of growth. It is no easy feat to accept what you cannot change, and it is no easy feat to explore yourself in those moments - the light, vulnerabilities, shadows, insecurities, fears, and so on. I am thankful for this journey of vulnerability that has led me to explore more of who I am and ultimately, who I want to be.

You use this pain, instead of dwelling on it. Why sabotage your lived experience with things you cannot control?

With this awareness, you realize the irony in the fact that no matter what, everything is in alignment even when it is out of your control. The universe is a friendly space that supports, loves, and nourishes you even when you are unaware - trust is necessary. Your path is yours. What happens is meant to be.

You think that can sometimes feel like a cop-out but it is always true and you know that. How would you know how things should and shouldn't work on a grand scale? You can barely see past your own limited perspective in everyday life. In the process of defending yourself from a small portion of the world, you can miss out on the larger world, full of so much goodness. Closing yourself off to that would be a pity.

You remember that the universe is a friendly space that supports, loves, and nourishes you even when you are unaware. This has most definitely been your experience thus far. Why would that change now? Once again, trust is necessary.

Be grateful for these moments. Do not let your emotions mask the beauty of life. Do not project your insecurities into your life experience. Do not die to your experience with self-inflicted suffering. Instead, engulf yourself in them with an inward focus and wait for them to pass. As with everything, this too (whatever it may be) shall pass. Indeed, it will.

In the meantime, live here now; be here now - where else would you be? Would you rather remain in your thoughts, narratives, and emotions? It's clear that those spaces have left you in a frenzy and whirlwind, just to return back to the same circumstance. Observing the circumstance with an awareness of your vulnerability allows for a certain openness in your response. Showing up in this way in itself gives the circumstance less power. The power now resides in you. You are back in *control*. Your awareness and focus shifts the experience completely. Maybe you focus on your internal reality (your triggers, the source of your emotions, etc. like previously stated) or the external conditions that affect you directly and those that don't.

In a vulnerable moment like going through a pandemic stuck in a foreign country, you might say things like (taken from a 2020 journal):

I need to be grateful for these moments. I need to honor this leg of my journey. I need to be present, aware, and fully here. I need to live these moments just as much as I dislike them. I have to make the most of these moments because whether I like it or not, this is my life. No matter how hard it is to believe, you are here because you are meant to be here.

I am going to try to maintain my gratitude for all that I have here and now. All of my needs are met. I am in a comfortable place. I have my health, shelter, clothing, friends, and food. I am able to provide for myself and offer myself some of my desires. I am very grateful. Thank you, Universe.

I am thankful to be alive and learn from this experience. I am learning so much. I am growing so much and I am so grateful. Thank you, Universe. Thank you so much! The human experience is so varied and diverse. I am on my path, seeking and finding what works for me, figuring out how I want to live this experience.

I am blessed. I understand that this thing called life is a joint venture. The Universe and I (as one ultimately) are working together for my greater unfoldment. I am attracting. I am seeking. I am met with obstacles, opportunities, connections, problems, confusion - all for my higher purpose and unfoldment. I am thankful for the teaching moments of discomfort.

It seems that vulnerability in vulnerable times pushes you into thanksgiving, or maybe this is simply an exercise to get out of your small circumstance or limited perception. Nonetheless, it works. From an inner awareness of your triggers and tensions to a grander awareness of your grace and favor, adventures in vulnerability are just that, an adventure. It doesn't have to be a chore or burden; it is life. And through it, you reach higher heights. Being open to life on all fronts even when it's uncomfortable is to live life fully, wholly, and boldly.

You reflect on your journey to this awareness with humor; so crazy how you lose yourself in your mind and are then reintroduced to the bliss of being you, the bliss of life. What a weird experience. Why would one willingly go through that?

And in the end, you realize we are all experiencing the same thing differently. It is called life. Life takes a level of vulnerability and openness and any hesitation and reluctance can simply ruin the beauty of the experience.

About the Author

lavasjah shabre' is a nomadic, planetary citizen, inspiring to make a difference in the world by fully and authentically living while inspiring others to do the same. Having visited each continent (excluding Antarctica) by the age of twenty-four, lavasjah shabre' is a self-proclaimed student of the world and an advocate for open hearts, minds and living. She has spent the last ten years in a trifecta of academia, work and travel in pursuit of the fullest expression of life and being. With a Bachelor's and Master's in Communication and Communication Management as well as training in yoga, meditation and life coaching, she founded the newly formed platform nothing&everything that explores the inherent stillness and fullness of life. She hopes to encourage others to live authentic, full lives through personal expression, self-introspection and self-actualization.

Website: nothingandeverything.co
Instagram: instagram.com/luhveyjh
Email: lavasjahcan@gmail.com

From Farm to Fork - Your Health is your Freedom

By Sinéad Téhéry Cronin

Inwardly I groaned as I watched my mother pull up in our little red van, blonde hair looking wild, matching the patchwork trousers and wellies she had obviously adorned in the garden only minutes before.

Her French accent reached me before she did as she greeted the other parents waiting outside the traditional primary school, mostly mothers who drove relatively new cars and wore full faces of makeup.

They may have all been there for the same reasons yet in this conservative little Irish village, our family was certainly a little out of the norm.

My parents worked the land, running an organic market garden business together for many years. My mother French and my father Irish, he was the black sheep of the family, donning a long beard and even longer hair. Having married a foreigner after choosing to attend a horticultural college he took up a way of life that was already becoming unfashionable. When he was inspired by 'new' (old) methods of farming that were in use in the Netherlands, people thought he was mad to choose to grow crops without the aid of chemical sprays and fertilizers; organic was not the well-known term it is today.

We moved to the village in which I was brought up when I was a year old. My parents took over a year to move a working market garden from the west of the county, where the land was poor, to the east where they purchased seven acres of better land with a small cottage that was renovated over many years. It was a simple life spent working with the land.

In primary school, I was the first non-Catholic to attend. I was definitely the only one turning up with homemade brown bread sandwiches and healthy lunches, long before this became a precedent. I knew we lived differently yet understanding and growing to appreciate this has been a lifelong journey.

Photos of these early years often include a pushchair in the garden with baby (me) asleep or awake watching the goings-on. My familiarity with the garden is since birth, understanding our relationship to the passing seasons. Knowing the importance of watching the weather. Whole days being spent outdoors, sowing, planting, watering, nurturing, and finally harvesting, then delivering. Choosing our meals based on what was seasonal and in abundance, garden to fork in its crudest form. During my school holidays, I travelled around on delivery routes with my parents in our little red van. Helping carry the boxes of herbs or vegetables into wholesalers and then later in the day into five-star restaurants where the pastry chefs knew me and always had a treat to share.

Sounds idyllic and in many ways, it was. It's a joy to me that now my son gets to experience similar experiences on the same smallholding. His grandparents (my dad's second wife) performing the same tasks that I once enjoyed as a young child. Feeding the animals, walking the hills, and of course everything garden-related.

It had always been my dream to travel and when I finished school, I found myself working in the health food shop my mum was managing, saving my pennies to get overseas on the adventures I dreamt of relentlessly. I learned so much about food, food alternatives for intolerances and allergies, and using supplements during my time here. I received training from certain brands and quickly got clued in around simple things like caffeine, sleep, exercise, and the effects these are having on us as part of a whole picture. Even with staff discounts, it was an effort not to spend my entire pay packet before leaving the shop at the end of the week! Both my mum and I were vegetarians during this time.

After a few trips within Europe, short-lived due to limited funds, I was finally getting my big escape with no plans to return. A few weeks in south-east Asia travelling from Singapore, through Malaysia, and up through Thailand en route to Australia where I was to spend a year as a backpacker on a working holiday visa. What a year it was... fun, sunshine, travel, camping, new friends, and a lot of cheap beer and pizza. I found a lot of budget foods in Australia to be highly processed. Following that, came a year of travel in Asia, the beginning of a love affair with Cambodia where the pizza is cheap and the beer even cheaper! They also tend to use MSG in just about everything.

When I returned to the Australian west coast to join some friends working on a huge conventional vegetable farm, I was three sizes bigger, bloated, chubby, and spotty. The only time I have ever been overweight in my life. The work was physically strenuous. We worked long hours harvesting and as I consciously cut the majority of sugar and processed foods from my diet the weight began to fall off over the coming months. Yet some other symptoms remained and I went for my first food intolerance test. Sure enough, some foods I suspected showed up and this was the beginning of my journey with food intolerances, restrictions, testing, and consciously changing diet to assist and support the body.

In the following years, I continued to travel, mostly between Cambodia where I came to own a small seasonal clothing store on the beach and back to Australia to top up my funds! At times I was eating fully gluten-free yet other times choosing the cheap and easy options when it came to food.

I began to play with different ways of eating to see what suited me. I tried eating an anti-candida diet which is fully sugar-free, Paleo diet, Keto, low FODMAP and elimination diets. I grew a love for fermentation and had kefir grains which used to travel with me as I roamed - not very practical, I wouldn't recommend it! Over these years I attended a number of clinics and was often given conflicting advice or suggestions that were impractical for my lifestyle.

Through my own experimentation, I began to tune into my own individual needs and reaction to certain foods and in reflection, this has been such a huge part of my journey.

I returned to the vegetable farm a second time, this time feeling much more in alignment with healthy eating that suited me. With open eyes, I observed the quantities of chemicals being used on crops. From seedling to harvest each crop was being sprayed multiple times. I have stood in a field harvesting cabbage as the tractor sprayed crops growing in dead soil in the plot next door, tasting the chemicals as the wind blew it our direction. Observed my boss shout at us to leave the field when the automatic timer set the irrigation going over lettuce and we were being drenched in water filled with chemicals. Once we were harvesting broccoli that had fertilizer pellets recently spread, the heads would turn to mush in our fingers where the pellets had landed, yet this was boxed and went to supermarkets.

I gained perspective on the vast differences of farming on this scale to how I had been raised. My father was intrigued by the work I was doing and the machinery that was being used. Both farms were growing food for sale, and yet were worlds apart. My father practised biodynamic farming, taking organic to the next level by growing with the moon cycles and spreading organic preparations on the land to foster soil health. This was alongside other practices all of which the focus was to enhance soil health and give back to the soil more than was being taken. In comparison, the conventional setting was about turning over as large a crop as quickly as possible with no awareness of soil health. The man whose job it was to spray, recommended to his daughter-in-law with whom I worked, not to eat too many of the vegetables.

I began to get my food elsewhere. Choosing to purchase a weekly box of locally grown spray-free vegetables from the local town over taking vegetables home free of charge from the farm in which I worked. If I was stuck and did take anything home I would first soak it in vinegar water before consuming it. It struck me that food was either being grown for sustenance or being grown for profit.

Finding myself back in Ireland some years later, I joked with a friend about opening a raw food cafe based on a mutual passion for raw wholefoods, especially the sweet stuff! This evolved into my first food truck business and would be my career path over many years to come. Before it was a trend, I was attending markets and events selling veggie, vegan, raw and free from home-cooked wholefoods. Long days were spent in the kitchen experimenting with recipes, with early morning starts as I embraced the life of a market trader, towing my little food trailer around the country serving up containers of salads, nut roasts, soups and desserts to my growing number of loyal customers. More importantly, I was growing and sharing my passion for clean, homemade foods, using a lot of organic ingredients and becoming extremely proficient in the kitchen.

When I began to grow a little person in my belly it was time to give this business up as the hours and heavy lifting were not conducive to pregnancy and the early years of motherhood. Those early years took me on a rollercoaster with my health. The pregnancy was a thoroughly enjoyable experience, the birth challenging; though he was born at our home in a loving supportive environment, it was not long after the birth that my body went into shock.

Growing a baby really does deplete our body's stores: breastfeeding, lack of sleep and transitioning to parenthood are all challenging experiences in themselves. Unfortunately, birth can be for many a traumatic experience and it is my belief that all physical dis-ease within the body is connected to our emotions. I began to experience symptoms of thrush, migraines, brain fog, stomach pain and lumps to name a few. I was living in discomfort daily.

As he grew, I cut out sugar and returned to an anti-candida diet, feeling the need to detox yet being unable to or take any herbs as I continued to breastfeed. The doctors were mostly unhelpful, performing tests that did not give me any answers and telling me that I was fine when I very obviously wasn't. I was living in a state of constant irritability caused by my body being in constant discomfort. I remember lying on the floor with my five-month-old, playing with him, entertaining him, praying he would need a nap soon so we could go to bed, crippled with a migraine, full body ill, messaging my ex at work, begging him to come home early when I could cope no longer. Feeling like a failure. Struggling to cook, struggling to incorporate the foods that would support me. My body reacting badly to the foods I was eating. Getting any meal at all on the table was a win.

Feeling desperate, I went to a natural health clinic and had a number of expensive tests done. The food intolerance testing was helpful in identifying and eliminating triggering foods I had not been aware of, however when I returned for the second appointment with the clinic nutritionist I was disappointed to overhear her giving the exact same advice to the client ahead of me, a one-size-fits-all approach yet I knew that a plan that could work for one person was not necessarily the approach for me. They diagnosed me with candida overgrowth and recommended a number of herbs even though I had specified that I was breastfeeding. When I returned home and did my own research, I saw they were not safe to take; I felt at such a loss and this was the final straw in losing faith in health professionals. Once again, I felt totally alone in figuring out what the path to healing was for me. These were baby steps in easing my symptoms but I was a long way from being healed.

Shortly after, I realised that I was suffering from postnatal depression. I had been feeling isolated and unsupported as well as ill since my son had been born and it was time for a physical as well as an emotional move. I also sought professional support through counselling which helped greatly.

Just before my son's first birthday, I began to study part-time, ironically with my dad as he runs a hugely popular intensive course 'How To Be an Organic Market Gardener'. Here I had the opportunity to grow my skill set, meet like-minded people from around the country and was once again doing something which supported my passions. Our neighbour informed me of a part-time gardening job going at the local seed savers. I applied and got the job. Life morphed into the next phase, being a busy working mother and preparing nutritious meals was not always easy. It seemed the same challenges followed, how can I find the space in my day or week to get the meals I desire on the table to support my family's nutrition?

It was at this time I discovered batch cooking which is a useful tool for anyone who doesn't want to cook daily.

Balance of sorts was being resumed in my life and I was at a stage where I had learnt to live with my symptoms though they were constantly present.

It was only some time later when I left my relationship that I began to re-evaluate and ask myself questions like: Do I want to continue to live like this? What does healthy look like? Is it only filling my cupboards and fridge with healthy foods? Is it only food? How deeply is my emotional state connected to my physical health? What practices support my mental state? In turn, does this affect my emotional well-being?

How do I want to feel and how can I get there?

I took matters into my own hands. I began to look at my life as a whole and make changes. If I reverted into old habits or ways, my body screamed out in discomfort as a result of what was happening for me emotionally (what an eye-opener), or from foods which in turn helped me to identify what I was reacting to. Instead of placing the power into the hands of others and feeding the feelings of desperation, I decided to empower myself. I made the decision to heal myself. I researched different tests and decided what would be most applicable to my situation and give me scientific results to the questions I was asking (believe me, those lab results changed my life!)

I held the power. I tuned into my body, I listened to her wise voice. Those lab results confirmed some of what I felt from when I tuned in (but I had doubted myself) as well as showed me clearly what was happening within my body.

I worked with the results and all the knowledge I acquired through my life's journey to create a plan for myself, a lifestyle that suits me and my needs as well as fitting easily into my family life. It's strict where it needs to be strict and flexible when I need it to be flexible.

We are amazing. Our bodies are healing all of the time.

So many people are lost on the journey with their health, people who feel the need and desire for self-sovereignty. There are thousands if not millions of people who desperately want to feel healthy yet are stuck in overwhelm. Not knowing how to incorporate healthy foods into their busy schedule and lives, not knowing how to tune into their own bodies to feel into what is right for them, what supports them. It's a bigger picture, just as we must nurture a plant from seed to blooming, we must also be gentle and nurture ourselves.

This has now become my mission as a food and diet coach. To guide others to empower themselves, learning to listen to themselves, and with ease filling their and their families lives with nutritious healthy food that supports them in being healthy and thriving.

I have a free foodie Facebook group for people on all diets, in which we share wholefood recipes, have a community and get inspiration. You can join here:

www.facebook.com/groups/healthydietmadesimple

A final note on food -

Food comes from the earth, yet the majority of people purchase their food in a plastic packet off a supermarket shelf, much of which I consider questionable to call it food!

Food sovereignty has been a foreign concept before 2020 yet in the face of a global pandemic, it is suddenly a reality. People have begun to embrace new hobbies and reconsider their values; having a garden at home has become more commonplace, allowing us to return to a way of the past which was the norm for our grandparents or great grandparents. An appreciation for local and seasonal produce is growing.

Within this, I urge you, consider healthy as a whole, claim sovereignty of your health and claim sovereignty over your food. Buy local when possible, support that farmer down the road. Growing food is fun and provides great satisfaction. Living in an urban setting? Fill some window boxes. Living with outdoor space? Grow food, not lawns! Save your own seed and share the seed. Purchase seed from local seed saving organisations which are ensuring the continuation of heirloom and open pollination varieties. Consider organic choices that will support both you and the earth.

'We have neglected the truth that a good farmer is a craftsman of the highest order, a kind of artist'.
~ Wendell Barry

'You don't have to cook fancy or complicated masterpieces - just good food from fresh ingredients'.
~ Julia Child

About the Author

Sinéad Téhéry Cronin works as a Food and Diet Coach taking people from overwhelmed to healthy.

She grew up on an organic market garden in the west of Ireland, an environment where eating farm to fork was an everyday occurrence.

After healing her health through food and running her own hospitality business, she now helps others to change their diet and better their health, as a result: improving their life.

If you would like to get in contact with me, please feel free to add me on Facebook: www.facebook.com/sinead.t.cronin

Facebook Page: www.facebook.com/stcdietcoaching
Email: sineadteherycronin@gmail.com

The Solo Path to Motherhood

By Tania Panasewicz

I have been a mother for five years and still not a day goes by that I don't pause and reflect on the miracle that my children are here. I am still in awe of the woman who let go of her dreams of a two-parent family and built one on her own.

All my life I wanted to be a mother. I would envision my life with my child. They would be home-schooled and we would travel the world. We would make it our classroom and learn about it together.

What was always missing from the picture was the man who would make this happen. He was assumed but never had a form; he was somewhere in the background but never imagined on our travels. I should have paid more attention to that vision as the years rolled by.

Perhaps it was growing up in a single-parent family. My parents had a rough divorce when I was six. It was something I never wanted to replicate. It left me with the certainty that when it came to a life partner - I would never settle for someone who didn't meet all my requirements. And I had many.

Not that I hadn't seen positive examples of what a marriage could be - they just seemed few and far between. Every time I saw one of these supportive unions, I would add another attribute to my very long list.

And so it was. I went through life largely single. I was an expert in short-term relationships and holiday flings. My long-term relationships were few and far between. I could identify the thing that would eventually break us within a few months and easily allow the short-lived unions to fade out.

Aged thirty-six, I ended a three-year relationship largely due to the fact that I realised he would never want a family. He always had excuses, something else to accomplish. Time was ticking and I didn't have it to waste. I didn't want a best friend. I wanted a partner who wanted to be a father.

And so began two years of searching. Of trying to find a man who would tick all the boxes and then knock me up!

Dating is a soul-destroying pastime at the best of times. When you add in the pressure of your biological clock, it takes on a whole new levity. Finding someone to 'right swipe' becomes nearly impossible. I gave myself: So. Many. Rules...

1. NO alcohol allowed in any of the pics. (Future baby daddy is NOT a drinker!)
2. NO pics at sporting events. (He will not neglect us to watch sports every day!)
3. NO shirtless mirror selfies. (Do I even need to elaborate?)
4. NO pics with kids that he then hastily explains away as belonging to someone else! (Prob doesn't want his own?)
5. NO pics with mystery women. (Even if they're his sister - it's just weird!)

And then if he does pass the first set of hurdles and we match... a whole new set of rules:

1. Must not open with, 'hey!' or any other one-word greetings. I need a man who communicates!
2. Must not instantly ask for your phone number. (Let's see if we mesh first!)
3. Must ask and answer questions. (How hard is this?!)
4. If he has children, they MUST be prominent in his life. (Or how could I be assured he'd be a good dad to our kids!)
5. Must love to travel.

Suffice to stay, it was not an easy couple of years for me. At the end of it, I had a slew of crazy dating stories and one wonderful friend that I'm still close to. It wasn't all bad.

However, at age thirty-eight, I had finally accepted my reality; I was not going to meet Prince Charming. He was not lurking in the corners of my dating apps. He was not behind me in the checkout line at the supermarket and he most certainly was not taking up a seat at my bar, sipping on Bourbon. It was time to work out a way to make it happen on my own.

Love can wait. My fertility would not.

As women, we assume that our eggs will patiently await our life plan. That when we decide to start a family they will leap to action and produce the longed-for baby. That all we need to do is introduce sperm into the equation and wait nine months.

What I discovered is that we are woefully under-informed about the realities of the reproductive system and its very real shelf life.

Becoming a mother by using a sperm donor had been in the back of my mind since my early thirties. It was my back up plan to my back up plan. The emergency fund I had hoped to never have to spend. Reaching the decision to become a Single Parent by Choice was not an easy one.

I had to grieve the dream of a partnered family. I had to let go of the idea of knowing the man behind the genetics of my child or children. I found it incredibly hard to let go.

I felt like a failure. What was wrong with me that I was incapable of finding love? Why was I so adept at finding men who could not commit to having families? Who on earth CHOOSES to bring a child into the world ON THEIR OWN! It went against all of the societal norms that are absorbed by us since infancy.

I worried about what would happen to my children when they grew up. Would they hate me for having them without a father? How would their futures be affected by this decision that had been made without their consent? I worried about what people would think of me. How would I answer probing questions about my kids' origin story?

It was only after I was introduced to a Single Mother by Choice who was about to give birth to her first child that I began to let go of my grief and see this as my path too. She was amazing. She was giving and kind. She answered all of my questions patiently. We became friends and I finally was able to let go of my grief and my guilt and begin my journey towards motherhood.

What I realised was that the person who had judged me the harshest and had been holding me back the most was myself. I was standing in the way of my own happiness. The second I had this a-ha moment, I was able to let go of my fears and embrace whatever was to come.

And so began the toughest three years of my life.

I thought choosing a sperm donor would be incredibly hard but it turns out that after years of internet dating I was pretty good at swiping left. I had a pretty simple list of requirements. A minimum height, good family health history, a strong jawline and someone who wasn't overly religious. Adult pictures were non-negotiable. I needed to see that the cute kid grew into a normal looking man. And he had to look like someone I might have dated. It was time consuming to wade through all of the profiles but choosing a donor was a lot easier than I thought.

Making my body do its part was not as easy.

Outwardly there appeared to be no good reason why pregnancy was alluding me. I had good fertility stats for my age. I was healthy with clockwork cycles.

They investigated deeper and it was discovered that I only have half a uterus. (A unicornuate uterus.) Only one of my ovaries was attached to my uterus which meant that I had to be ovulating from that side for any reasonable chance of success. For some reason, women with this anomaly often have a harder time conceiving.

I decided my best chance at having a child was to move to IVF.

IVF is not cheap and was NOT covered under my insurance policy. Correction. It was covered but only if you were MARRIED! What kind of draconian BS is that! I met all the criteria for infertility coverage except for the wedding band.

I had to get creative in order to make this happen. Extra shifts at work, loans, 0% interest credit cards, a line of credit. All of these (and my savings) were utilised in my quest for a baby.

IVF is not easy. Daily injections, early morning appointments, internal ultrasounds, surgeries and constant worry.

My first round of IVF was very successful on paper. Out of eight eggs retrieved, four made it to blastocyst. That's a five-day-old embryo that is considered a healthy candidate to become a human baby!

Due to my only having half a uterus, it was decided that I could only transfer one at a time because of the risk of twins.

So that's what I did. And each time it didn't work. Nothing. Stark white pregnancy tests and a sympathetic nurse telling me it didn't work this time.

At this point, I had spent $25,000 and had nothing to show for it except for a full sharps' container, a broken heart and a very real sense of fear.

What had I done? Had I waited too long and sabotaged my own dream? I was mad at every man I'd wasted time dating when I knew it wouldn't lead anywhere. I was mad for trying so hard to find a partner when all I had ever wanted was the child. I was furious at myself.

I knew I had to try again. You can always make more money. You can't always have a child. I could live with debt but I couldn't live without a child. It's not an ideal way to bring a human into the world but I knew I would make it work.

I went back for a second round of IVF and changed donors. Maybe the first one hadn't been compatible with me. My RE said it was worth a try. It was one of the positive aspects of doing this on your own.

As I sat waiting for my egg retrieval a nurse came in. She said cheerily to me, 'It always works on the third time!' I wanted to punch her squarely in the nose as I replied, 'This is my second time.' I felt as though it was already doomed.

But once again I had great numbers and another five blastocysts. My RE was very confident that the good one would be in there. We transferred two!

Negative. It didn't work.

I was devastated but still had three embryos on ice. That had been my fifth embryo transfer and it didn't make sense! The embryos looked perfect. We did more testing but it revealed nothing.

I'd been doing acupuncture, drinking fertility smoothies, cut out coffee, gluten and anything that might possibly have a negative effect on my chances. I was out of ideas.

Then I was referred to a woman who specialises in Mayan Abdominal Massage. It was worth a shot. She had an excellent reputation and had helped a lot of women finally achieve pregnancy.

It was strange but amazing. I could really isolate and feel where my uterus was during the massage and connected deeply with it afterwards too. I felt like something had shifted. I went into my next transfer with a little more confidence than usual.

We put two more embryos in and I waited. For the first time ever, I decided to test early and for the first time ever, two pink lines appeared on the stick! I was pregnant! It was a miracle! I was overjoyed!

Two weeks later I went for an ultrasound to see the baby's heartbeat. My mother came with me. I knew immediately that something was wrong. She was taking too long. She had gone too quiet. I said, 'It's bad isn't it? There's no heartbeat. I've been in this world long enough to know that if there's no heartbeat that this isn't a viable pregnancy.' She answered this was probably the case but to wait and talk to the doctor.

He was solemn. He said to wait a week to be sure. To remain 'pessimistically optimistic' but that the chances were very, very small that this would correct itself.

I worked that whole week knowing a dead thing was inside me. I needed the distraction but I felt as though my world was ending. I was out of money, out of energy and almost out of hope.

The D & C was one of the worst days of my life. I cried all day. My dream felt like it had ended. I didn't want the pregnancy to end but I also couldn't wait for it to be over. It is still hard to talk about it now.

I took a break. I needed it desperately.

I somehow managed to see the positive in the loss. I knew that it had been a chromosomal abnormality and wasn't compatible with life. But on the positive side this had proven that my uterus could become pregnant! So, if I had a compatible embryo, surely I could actually create life from it?

I still had one embryo but I knew I couldn't mentally cope with the trauma of another loss. I decided that I would do one more round of IVF and this time I would test *all* of the embryos to greatly reduce that risk. I still had the nurse's words in my head, 'It always works on the third time!'

I selected a new donor. It took fifteen minutes. I was a pro at filtering them out by now. I was also just going through the motions.

I got three blastocysts. I was older and it showed. Off they all went to be genetically tested.

I was on my way to my end-of-season work party when I got the news. We were about to board a boat for the sunset sail. One embryo had passed the testing! It was one more than I expected! As I watched the sun set on the water, surrounded by friends, I felt hope for the first time in years.

I ate healthily, did abdominal massage and three months later I transferred my brightest hope into my body. Five days later I saw what I'd been hoping for... two pink lines! My baby boy had gotten cosy!

I was delighted and I was terrified. After a loss you are never able to fully enjoy your pregnancy. You have experienced the worst-case scenario and you want to protect your heart from the pain of it again. You also want to be a happy home for the growing life inside of you. It's an internal struggle but for me thankfully happiness won.

At five weeks, five days, after a bleeding scare (because of course there had to be drama!) I saw my son's heartbeat for the first time. What an amazing sight. It was so strong, so early. The nurse told me, 'You've got a fighter in there, you don't need to worry!'

At thirty-nine weeks and a very uneventful pregnancy I delivered my perfect little boy into the world. I was a mother at last. There are no words that exist to describe how elated I was and have continued to be that he is here.

My story doesn't end there. When he was fourteen-months-old, I decided to do it all over again. Being a mother was so enjoyable that I wanted to grow our family. And the law had changed. Now single women were entitled to fertility treatments so I wouldn't need to go as deeply into debt.

Again, my journey was not straightforward. Three rounds of IVF produced only one embryo which did not take. I knew in my core that I was no longer capable of producing a genetic child and was not prepared to put my body through any more cycles. I decided to stop and be happy as a parent of an only child. I was satisfied that I had at least tried.

Then my friend stepped forward and offered me her embryos. We had used the same donor (which is how we knew one another) and her family was complete. After much talking, therapy, lawyers and excitement, two tested embryos were flown across the country in a snowstorm to my clinic. What a journey they had been on already.

The first one didn't work. It was a huge blow. I was so confident that it would. Back to the massage therapist I went.

The second embryo snuggled in and is now my beautiful daughter! My family was at last complete.

And all of those worries I had? Gone! I no longer feel like a failure for not having provided my children with a father. Families come in all shapes and sizes and procreating with a real-life man is no guarantee of his presence or positive role modelling in your child's life.

Will my children resent me? Who knows, all teenagers are mad at their parents at some point about something. Maybe I have a head start because I know what that thing could be! I lead with honesty and empathy. I do my best to teach my children how to be good communicators. We talk about everything. We read books that help them grasp the subject. They will never know any different. My children know how babies are made (in a Petri dish of course) and what with (sperm, an egg and a uterus).

How do I answer questions about their origin stories? With honesty (where appropriate.) My comfort in their stories will be absorbed by them so it's the only way. And if anyone probes deeper than I'm comfortable with, I tell them that I'm not comfortable with answering. After all it's my children's story and I save the details for them alone to share.

And now I use the knowledge I have gained to help others who want to start families on their own. I help them navigate the pitfalls and avoid making the mistakes that I made on my own journey. I instil them with the confidence to become single parents by choice. I help them grieve the life plan that they had imagined and move forward to one that will guarantee their happiness. And if it doesn't happen for them easily, I mentor them through infertility also. I do this via one-to-one mentoring and in group programs.

If you would like to learn more or work with me, you can find me in any of these places. Mention you heard about me through this book and I will give you a free thirty-minute session and send you my free PDF on how to choose a sperm donor!

About the Author

Tania Panasewicz is an Entrepreneur and Single Mother by Choice. At age thirty-eight, Tania decided to stop searching for Prince Charming and build a family via sperm donation! After battling infertility for three years she welcomed her son in 2016. Her daughter was conceived via embryo donation three years later. Tania now uses her experiences to mentor single women through their fertility journeys.

Website: www.fertilitymentoring.com
Facebook Page: www.facebook.com/thefertilitymentor
Facebook Group: www.facebook.com/groups/smcsupportgroup
Email: fertilitymentoring@gmail.com

Lose The Fear and Transform Your Birth: Tales From a Midwife

By Linsy Brito

"I can't do this.

I'm frightened.

I can't take the pain.

Am I going to die?

Help me, please!"

The words that echo inside birth rooms around the world. The day a woman brings new life into the world. The most painful and scary day of her life!

Fear, anxiety and pain take root. As birth approaches you willingly hand over the reins of your birth to a professional who knows what they are doing, because you don't? Maybe this is the first sacrifice of motherhood?

But a woman's body, your body, is designed to birth your baby.

Your baby doesn't need help to grow. You relinquish control and let it grow. Likewise, your baby doesn't need help to be born. Your body and your baby instinctively know what to do.

So why does the thought of giving birth send chills through most pregnant women?

Maybe because generations of increasing medicalization of birth and the media portrayal of birth suggests it is deeply traumatic, painful and dangerous have burrowed deep into our subconscious. The belief that we need help to birth our baby, unlike all other mammals on Earth, and it will be agony. This is not how evolution designed our entry to motherhood.

I have been a midwife my whole adult life. I eat, sleep and breathe birth and I love it!

I want you to know that birth isn't just something you have to endure. It's your body, your baby, your birth. We can't control birth, but your mindset, preparation and the decisions you make through pregnancy all impact how your birth unfolds.

Your birth should be an empowering and positive experience, not something you try hard to forget.

People assume that a pregnant midwife has all the answers. We must know what we're doing, right? Well, it's a blessing and a curse. The more we know, the more there is to worry about. And a funny thing happens when a midwife has a baby. All the knowledge and logical decision-making capability evaporates. Firstly, baby brain, because that shit's real! Secondly, because once that baby is growing inside of you, you are a mum and not a midwife.

The birth of my first daughter was pretty standard. I agreed to be induced at thirty-seven weeks. The fluid around her was low and she was pretty small. I knew I wanted a natural birth (well as close as possible) and no epidural so I could stay mobile.

I was giving birth in the hospital where I worked. I knew where I was going, the room I would be in, the people that would look after me and exactly what would happen. But still I was petrified! I couldn't sleep at all the night before. My stomach was churning. How was I going to get through this? I'd seen the pain of induction. I'd seen how it can take days with no sleep. I'd reassured women as they cried on my shoulder about how they would never have the energy to push a baby out after three days of no sleep. Now it was my turn and I was frightened.

We arrived on the ward at 8am sharp and the process got underway. I was expecting the pain but not the speed with which the contractions began. The room was so small. My God, I didn't know where to put myself! I just knew I couldn't stay in the same position for more than a couple of contractions. I wasn't even classed as being in labour yet!

My husband didn't know what to do or say to me either. This was completely new for him. He sat watching me writhe around in pain, feeling helpless. This went on for hours. I wanted to try a nice hot bath to relax. I left the security of my little room and walked out into the corridor in the middle of visiting time. I weaved my way in and out of all the people as my senses were assaulted by the noise and the bright lights. I just needed to make it to the bathroom before another contraction dropped me to my knees. I had never felt so vulnerable.

But the 'sanctuary' of the brightly lit, clinical bathroom, didn't bring me the comfort I'd hoped. I couldn't fit my belly in the tiny bath no matter how I tried. Being laid on my back when the next contraction hit was intolerable.

I scuttled back to my tiny room with very little pacing space. I needed drugs! I tried gas and air along with an opiate injection that didn't even touch the sides. I remember rocking on my hands and knees. The same chatter racing through my mind with each and every contraction "Oh my God, it's coming again, I won't survive another contraction, am I going to die?" Not a good mantra to be repeating over and over. But I was quiet. Despite all the irrational thoughts running through my mind, to the outside world, I was 'coping' well. That word is used so often in maternity. As women, we must find a way to 'cope with' birth. Shouldn't the birth of our baby be a cherished experience rather than an event we must endure?

I admitted defeat and faced up to the fact that an epidural was my last option. An hour later I lay half propped up in bed. Dead from the waist down but comfortable and pain-free. Now the effects of the opiate injection really kicked in. I couldn't keep my eyes open and found it almost impossible to communicate. But I could hear the world around me. I knew there was concern about my baby's heart rate and that she was in an awkward position for birth. I could hear the *dum dum dum* of the heart rate monitor next to me. My midwife's brain was tuned in to the slowing of her heart rate from time to time, but I didn't have the energy to open my eyes. I felt safe though. My friends were taking care of me and I trusted them completely.

It was soon time to push. I had no feeling whatsoever, so it took a bit of practice to get it right. The classic saying 'leave your dignity at the door' could not have been more prominent than at that moment.

Knees bent, legs open, grab the back of my legs, chin on chest, deep breath, no noise, push until I run out of breath, snatch a breath and do it again. All while everyone in the room has their eyes squarely focused on my vagina. Strangely, I was more concerned with how my pushing face looked. All screwed up, red and sweaty. Stoned on drugs and with no pain or pressure to think about, my mind was free to worry about much less important things.

But the clock was ticking. Hospital protocols dictate that labour must progress according to the clock and my time was up. The consultant was called in to 'give me a hand' and my legs were placed into the stirrups, hanging limply like dead weights. I pushed with everything I had. I wanted a natural birth! No forceps and no episiotomy (the dreaded cut down there). Just as the consultant arrived on the ward, a child was born. Out she came, with her cone head and bruised face, but crying and full of life. I had done it myself!

I didn't think too much about my birth experience, not in a negative way anyway. Not until I was pregnant again. Then it suddenly hit me! I DID NOT want to feel like I did the first time. I couldn't put my finger on it, to begin with. I wanted a natural birth and I got one. Healthy mum and a healthy baby. So why was my mind screaming at me that it needed to be different?

My birth was pretty standard. I was induced. Epidural. Progressed quickly. My baby was continuously monitored which meant I was attached to a monitor the whole time. I had a vaginal birth, a tear, stitches.

It was the usual medicalized and conveyor belt system of care. The one-in, one-out, type births that happen in maternity units throughout the world. So why did the prospect of doing it again feel so scary and uncomfortable?

I thought about it long and hard. I realized that I had felt so vulnerable and so exposed. So scared and in so much pain. So out of control. The lack of confidence to make my own decisions was overwhelming. Worst of all... feeling like I was going to die! How could I contemplate going there again?

I expressed my fears to a midwife friend who suggested a home birth. I was shocked! With all that can go wrong! I'd had the privilege of being present for some beautiful home births over the years but never considered it for myself. Not for me!

But the seed was planted. I discussed it with my husband who wasn't sure. He was concerned about the safety aspect if something were to go wrong, and the mess of course. The same two objections most partners have. But he trusted my reasoning and judgment and happily participated in the excitement of planning our homebirth.

My friend also suggested a hypnobirthing course. The idea didn't fill me with excitement to begin with. I didn't know in detail what it was. The name conjures up visions of stage hypnosis and pocket watches. I definitely didn't want anyone hypnotizing me and I doubted I could be hypnotized anyway.

But I wanted a homebirth. I thought I was going to die during my contractions last time, and I wouldn't be getting an epidural at home. I knew in my heart there must be a better way. So I decided to hire a pool to help me relax in labour and booked in for hypnobirthing. I was willing to try anything to make this birth better.

Hypnobirthing is birth education and preparation. As well as lots of practical tools and techniques, you will learn how your body and baby work together for birth, birth hormones, place of birth, birth environment. How to evaluate the benefits and risks of interventions so you can make informed decisions with your doctor or midwife. It does not mean a pain-free birth, although there are stories of women who have achieved this. But it can reduce the perception of pain based on the fear-tension-pain cycle. The more fear, the more tension, the more pain is experienced.

Reducing fear with knowledge and understanding, along with relaxation techniques can reduce tension, which in turn can reduce pain.

So, I listened to the guided meditations, affirmations and practiced my breathing. When the big day arrived, I was ready.

It was 8am on a warm Summer morning and the sun was shining on me through the large patio doors of my living room. I was weightless and swaying in the warm water, a final moment of calm. I began to feel the surge inside me, the pressure strengthening. Was this the last one before I was finally able to meet my baby? My body gave one final almighty push and... release. I gently brought my baby up and out of the water. I did it! I was elated! I had my family all around me, including my two children, exactly the way I had visualized the birth of my baby. It's a girl!

My daughter was sitting on my husband's knee with a little wrapped gift in her hand. She was waiting patiently to open her mound of presents on the coffee table on the other side of the birth pool. That's why this was day even more special. It was her fourth birthday and her first present of the day was her new baby sister.

Our tiny baby was so calm, so peaceful. Lying on my chest in the warm water with her eyes open. The feelings of relief, love and pride all rushing through me.

Our ten-year-old son had the proud job of cutting the cord. It was heart-warming to see my children so involved in the birth of their sister.

An hour later the pool was gone, the room was clear and I was sat breastfeeding my tiny new baby as my other daughter was shrieking with delight as she opened her birthday presents. This was exactly how I had envisioned it. I'd had a feeling for weeks that she would be born on the same day as her sister.

The surges had started a few hours before. I walked around and around in the early hours while everyone slept. The chatter inside my mind was very different from last time, thanks to the mindset preparation and practice I had done. This time, through each surge, I was repeating an affirmation - "my surges cannot be bigger than me because they are me". I rearranged the room, prepared the birth pool, then decided around 3am to wake my husband.

A massive part of hypnobirthing is the role of the birth partner. My husband now knew what I needed from him, emotionally and physically. Logistically, he knew his jobs were to keep the pool topped up with hot water and the tea and biscuits flowing to the midwives. This was a world away from him sitting helplessly in the corner of my hospital room like last time.

He was an amazing support. By 5am he suggested we should call the midwife. I worried it was too early. Being a midwife, I knew I didn't want to get my friends and colleagues out of bed for nothing! He assured me he thought it was time. By 6am I was submerged in the warm water. That immediate relaxation you feel as you lower yourself into a hot bath. Heaven!

This experience changed everything for me. I felt strong and powerful. Confident and so proud of myself.

This is how all women should feel as they bring new life into the world.

I wanted to share what I had learned with women everywhere. The year after my home hypnobirth I signed up and got certified to teach.

Even before starting to teach full hypnobirthing courses, I immediately started sharing some of the techniques with the women I cared for in the hospital and the way I practised changed.

I recognized, and put a stop to, the unnecessary chatter in the birth room. Yes, it's important to build a rapport with a woman and her birth partner in a relatively short space of time, but there comes a point when small talk should stop. I stopped coaching women to actively push unless absolutely necessary. No more quick vaginal examinations to make sure her cervix was fully dilated if she had urges to push. Instead, I would teach her how to breathe effectively so she could work with her body. I became the ultimate protector of her birth space, knowing and ensuring her primal and instinctual needs of a quiet, calm and dimly lit space were met. Even small changes at a crucial time could make a massive impact on their birth experience.

I have given birth twice since becoming a hypnobirthing midwife and mum. Two very different births, but hypnobirthing techniques gave me the strength and the mindset I needed.

My third daughter was born asleep at nineteen weeks. I was induced and gave birth quickly and painlessly, with only three surges. I had spent the previous two days visualising the birth and repeating affirmations. I strongly believe this helped me through this devastating time. You can read more about that here lifeinthemotherhood.com/mia-birth-story

My fourth pregnancy I wanted to be surrounded by my family in the comfort and safety of my own home again. But of course, things don't always go to plan and that's ok. My waters released early morning, but my surges never came. The following day I opted for induction. I used my hypnobirthing techniques, visualisations and affirmations and had a drug-free natural birth. You can read more about that here: www.lifeinthemotherhood.com/india-birth-story

My birth stories are all very different and medical intervention was welcomed when needed. For those with access to the medics and the life-saving procedures available, how lucky we are. Because situations arise where we must intervene. Being open to and able to adapt to a changing situation is crucial.

Hypnobirthing is not just for women who want a natural birth or a homebirth. It is for any woman who wants a positive birth. It is for women who want to be in control of their birth. For women who want to be part of the decision-making process, so whatever is *done to* them is done with their full informed consent. Everyone wants a healthy mum and a healthy baby. That goes without saying. The decisions you make in pregnancy and birth can have a profound effect on how your birth unfolds. The tools and techniques and the knowledge gained, can help keep you calm and focused when you need to adapt. Learning how is the first step.

The language we use and hear about birth is so important too. Negative words feed into feelings of inadequacy and chips away at the subconscious mind. Phrases such as, "the baby is in the 'wrong' position, you're 'only' three centimetres dilated, 'failure' to progress" and "'failed' induction" all feed into the notion that medical science needs to rescue women from their inadequate bodies.

This is what makes the mindset work so important during pregnancy and the lead up to birth. Almost every pregnant woman has been told a horror story. How much blood someone lost. How many stitches she had. How she'll never cope with the pain so just go straight for the epidural. This is the time to say no. No negative birth stories please, only positive ones. Once you've had your own birth experience, you'll be more than happy to swap stories.

Have you considered a birth plan? This can be quite a conversation piece too. A necessity to some, a complete waste of paper to others. But what other massive life-changing event would you build up to for nine months and put no plan in place?

A wedding, a house move, a holiday. They all require planning.

Sometimes plans don't work out and we need to go with the flow and adjust, but we begin with a plan and a vision all the same. Why should the birth of your baby be any different! It's okay to know what kind of birth you want, look into the ways in which you can help yourself achieve that birth. The birth place, the birth space, the people around you, the atmosphere, the mindset, the language used, your right to question things, discuss your options and be part of the decision-making process.

And if things don't go to plan, that's fine. Go with the flow. Everyone wants a healthy mum and a healthy baby. Elements of your plan may need to change. Other elements that are important to you can still be accommodated. Ultimately you want to give birth to your baby and look back on the experience positively, regardless of whether it went 'to plan' or not.

Your birth experience stays with you forever. The way you feel stays with you forever. Birth can't be fully controlled but it doesn't mean you are powerless.

You should follow your path towards the birth you choose, change course if need be, doing so because you understand how and why, giving birth to your baby by whatever means, and feeling happy with the end result. This is what makes an empowering birth experience. The feeling of being Superwoman despite needing a caesarean section when you planned a homebirth.

Because you know what? You are Superwoman! Your body just made a whole new human being. So what if your birth plan changed! You can't control everything. You are confident that your midwife and doctor did right by you and your baby. You adapted to the situation. You felt calm and in control. And you gave birth to your baby on your terms!

That is empowerment!

That is how all women should feel as they hold the precious new life they created close to them as you smell that addictive scent of your newborn baby. You should begin your motherhood journey feeling strong, confident and powerful.

You are not alone when you feel scared about birth, or when you believe the pain will be unbearable. Or when you worry that something bad may happen to you or your baby in this scary world of birth.

But I'm here to tell you that you don't have to feel this way. You don't have to walk this unknown path alone, feeling scared, lost, or isolated, wondering why this feels so hard despite thousands of women giving birth every day.

You can strive for the birth you desire, or as close as possible.

You can learn how well designed for birth your body actually is. You can gain the confidence to ask questions and make your own choices.

You can feel empowered by your birth.

You can actually enjoy your birth!

You just need someone to show you how. To listen to you, to teach you and to support you. As a midwife, a birth coach and a mother, I can help you. With the birth of every baby is also the birth of a mother. I want to help empower as many mothers as possible.

I work with women to prepare them for birth and those early days of motherhood too. Let's face it, newborns don't come with a handbook either.

If you are interested in hypnobirthing and would like a free taster session of my Birth Empowered Coaching Program you can get instant access here: www.linsybrito.com

If you would like to know more about my full Pregnancy to Postpartum Support Package, or book onto the Birth Empowered Program, you can find further details and contact me here: https://linsybrito.com/work-with-me

About the Author

Linsy Brito is a Midwife, Birth Coach and mum of four. She has spent the last twenty years as a midwife, devoted to caring for women through the transformative journey of birth and motherhood. Also as an experienced Hypnobirthing Teacher and a Certified Holistic Health and Nutrition Coach, she has merged her passions and experience into her role as a birth coach, providing a personalized and continuous support during pregnancy and postpartum. She provides mums-to-be with a safe space to learn, gain confidence and make their own decisions so they can step into their power to birth with ease. By helping women release fear and anxiety, they can achieve a calm and empowered birth experience and begin their motherhood journey feeling healthy, strong and confident.

Website: www.linsybrito.com
Facebook Page: www.facebook.com/midwifelinsy
Facebook Group:
www.facebook.com/groups/natutalpregnancyandbirth
Instagram: www.instagram.com/midwifelinsy
Email: linsy@linsybrito.com

From Fear To Freedom: Overcoming Post Natal Depression And Anxiety

By Nikki Sawyer

'You're making your baby sad'. That's what I was told as I sat heavily pregnant, in a cold clinical room in a hospital, pouring out my heart to a health practitioner. It was my third baby and every minute since the positive pregnancy test result had felt like a huge challenge. Gosh, to write these words is hard I must admit. Is my baby girl going to actually read them one day? I feel it's important to state that I love her so much, I love all three of my babies; I would kill for them, die for them and I wouldn't change a thing about my life and motherhood. My journey into motherhood has been a tough one though and I am sure many of you reading my words will relate. Since doing what I do and working with such amazing and brave women all over the world, the realisation is that we all have many things in common; mainly it's fear, anxiety and mum guilt.

On reflection, looking back at the beginning of motherhood, I fall down into a deep black endless hole of scenarios, situations and challenging times. Yet, I look at my children today and I am bursting with pride, love and happiness. Life can be so cruel. My mental health robbed me of my first years with my youngest princess. Those beautiful fat baby rolls, the smiles and the pink frilly baby dresses were all a blur. Instead of embracing this time, I felt pure guilt, sadness and despair. Don't get me wrong, there were some flashes of smiles sometimes, but most of the time it was dark, lonely and isolating. I was screaming for help yet not making a sound. I was too scared, I was ashamed and fearful of being labelled as a s**t mother, not a good wife and told that I couldn't do this. The thing is, I couldn't do this. Not this time and not in this way. I needed help.

I started out motherhood as a single mum. It was just my boy and me. He's a gem; I am so proud of the young man he is becoming and he is my best friend (all my kids are my best friends). You would think that in this situation, a single mother, no father figure for my son and trying to do everything myself would have caused my depression and issues with anxiety, but it didn't. Yes, it was hard and yes, the responsibility was massive, but it was also empowering. I worked, I looked after my son and I ran my own house. Life was okay! When my son was three, I met my Mr Darcy, my hubby (I love Pride and Prejudice by the way!) What an amazing man. He swept me off my feet (after I had kissed a few frogs!) and boom, I fell in love. Do you know what happened next?

He fell in love with my boy too! That was it, we were a family, my boy had a daddy and I had found my man. Life was getting good.

As you do when you fall in love, you make plans and move forward. Soon we had a house together and talked about having a baby. Before I knew it, our first little Sawyer princess was born. Man, was she a cutie (nine pounds six ounces of cuteness I might add, ouch!) It was amazing; our family felt complete and whole. I felt like I had everything I had dreamed of, the Cinderella story if you like! (God damn Disney though for getting in ya head and setting your sights so big!) There were some bumps along the way, of course. This isn't a Disney movie, after all, it's normal everyday life. I had been so used to parenting by myself, I had my own challenges; letting go of stuff and working as a team, but we found our flow, and all was ok. The usual sleep deprivation was a killer; I am vicious if I don't get eight hours at least, so that smarted a little! I was concerned that my boy would feel left out (he never did). So I did my utmost to split my time, ensure he was part of everything once home and that my days were all about the baby while he was in school. I had a balance. Where was my self-care time, though? Ermmm, I didn't have any! Yet, it didn't seem to bother me as much as it does now. Self-care is massive and something you will hear me talk a lot about further on! The conversation of more children had happened a couple of times, and we were both on the fence with this one. Were we happy with the nuclear family set up? Yes, I thought we were.

I had lost the baby weight, gone back to work and things were getting easier as our princess got older. My son was flourishing in everything he was doing and there seemed to be a good balance in our bubble. However, we didn't rule out one more bundle of joy in the future, it was something that was in the back of my mind and I often felt that I wasn't quite ready to say 'no more children' and 'no more' to fresh baby squidgy cuddles. That said, when our baby girl reached one, boom, I fell pregnant again. It shocked me! She wasn't quite on the agenda so early and was a surprise, to say the least. I had planned a career change and enrolled on a new course to do so. I had got my ass back after months of Slimming World and giving up my chocolate, meh! I still couldn't laugh without peeing my pants though, but I was getting there with the pre-pregnancy bod! Being pregnant again made me feel like I wasn't ready to put all the weight back on, to not have a bash at my new career path, to go through being pregnant again so soon after just doing it all: morning sickness, exhaustion and worry. Then there was the actual realisation that we didn't have space or money for another Sawyer baby. I felt so overwhelmed and to be fair, as soon as the test was positive, things changed in my head instantly and I couldn't fix it.

Telling my hubby scared me, I knew he would be shocked and the way I was feeling made me nervous to tell him. That night he was quiet, I was quiet, we pondered everything over and over again in our minds. I still had a baby to look after and my five-year-old son, how was I going to do this while pregnant? How was I going to work still? I had been so sick with my daughter's pregnancy that I really didn't think I could do it again. I hate being sick, it's one of the worst things for me; I cry a lot and can barely function. I had so many questions, scenarios and uncertainty. Then the mum guilt, anxiety and fear got me, girls. That's when it all started, and the s**t hit the fan.

The first eighteen months of my youngest daughter's life is a blur if I am honest. I have very few photos of myself, I couldn't even look at myself in the mirror. I couldn't find my flow; I had lost my identity and just went downhill from there. Let's jump ahead a little to the dark day, the turning point in my life that was my rock bottom, the day that I did not want to be here on planet earth anymore. Surely my kids deserved a better mummy than me? I was heavily medicated to try and cope with my postnatal depression, to find a way to function and that's exactly what the medication did. I just functioned. I struggled to get dressed and achieve anything in my day. If the kids were looked after and fed, I was pretty much done. Our everyday tasks felt huge, massive in fact, and I always felt overwhelmed and a complete failure before I even started.

I have a beautiful family picture of us all, it's in a national park here in the UK, a family day was planned, full of mud and giggles. Despite the fun-filled agenda, I was screaming and crying inside my head. I wanted to enjoy it, embrace my children and be grateful for what I had but I just couldn't. The day was a haze. It was a sunny day with a cool, fresh, crisp breeze. We had gone to stay with my mum and spend some time out of our usual mundane environment. A change of scene and a cuddle from my mum was definitely needed. We walked to the top of the park, up a peak, to admire the view. It was stunning. As my mum took the picture and said, 'say cheese', I just wanted to take a step back and fall off the peak we were stood on. I wanted it all to stop and go away. I didn't want to go back home, to what had become a prison cell and a place of darkness and anxiety. The only thing that stopped me stepping back and made me step forward was my kids. I couldn't do that to them.

No one would know a thing about my true emotional state to look at our family picture. We stood at the top of the peak with an amazing backdrop of blue sky, sunshine and trees. Everyone was smiling, including me, yet it was a horrific moment in my life. I still have this picture; I look at it a lot. I use it to reflect on my journey and how far I have come since then. I am not scared to look at it anymore. Yes, it makes me sad, but I have got a good handle on it now. I feel this guilt sometimes, for not being present for my youngest when she was so small due to my illness. I am happy to say though, that things have changed dramatically since this dark day. I could almost say I feel at peace with the first few years of her life and know that it wasn't my fault or hers. I love her so much and would be lost without her. We have a fantastic relationship and she knows nothing of how I felt.

The journey home on that terrible dark day was a quiet one. Once the kids were in bed, I broke down to my husband. I told him how I felt and how scared I was. I sobbed, hard, full-on, end of the world sobbed. To say it out loud and how real it had gotten scared me. My hubby was amazing, he just held me and reassured me. I cried myself to sleep but felt relieved. Finally saying to him I can't do this anymore and I need help was the step forward I needed to take, and I am so glad I did. I had held on to this all alone for so long, it wasn't healthy. The next day came; I felt drained and not sure what was coming next, but this was the first day of my positive journey forward. My support network came together, I talked, I crafted, and I got some perspective. We planned on how we could make things easier together, how we could make things lighter and how I could have the time to find myself again. Nikki was gone, I was just an empty shell and a small resemblance of who I used to be. The doctor just wanted to up my medication, but it got to the point where I was on the highest dose, there was nowhere else to go. I knew that at this point the change had to come from me. Only I could do things differently, no one was going to do it for me.

Finding yourself is the simplest thing to do, but as a mummy can be incredibly difficult. I had lost who I was. No one said my name, it was just constantly mummy, mummy, mummy or 'babe' from my hubby! I had no time to myself, no time to recharge and no time to be who I used to be before I became a mum. Who said in the rule book that once you become a mummy, your own life as the amazing individual you were, must end?! Why can't you have both? I had a long journey ahead of me, but it was a start and a huge step in the right direction.

Since then, five years ago, I have been able to turn a corner and find me again. With a lot of help and support from my family and friends I have overcome and dealt with my postnatal depression and got off the medication, I own the SOB! However, it has left me with anxious days and memories that I need to keep a handle on and deal with (I am not going to lie), but all in all, I did it, Boom!

How did I do it you ask? I spoke out and that's what I want YOU to do… talk to me. I learned to be me again and that it was okay to be me. I am not just a mum, a wife, I am ME. I am here for all women around the globe that feel like they want to hide away, step back off a big peak or feel unable to even wash the dishes. I learned the power of Neuro-Linguistic Programming (NLP), the magic from creative therapy and simple methods to create my very own anxiety tool kit to dip in and out of when needed.

TRUST me when I tell you, life does go on and you can blow those dark clouds away by finding yourself again, dealing with the scary emotions, making time for yourself and hitting those life goals (however big or small). Reach for the stars and smile at the sun, I'll be right there with you. I know you don't believe me; you are thinking as you read my words, 'what is she on? I don't have the time to get dressed let alone find time for myself or to reach for any form of life goal'. But trust me when I say, baby steps, in the right direction; how I did it WORKS. I want to help and share with you the 'how's' for making this happen. Obviously, everyone has different life goals, and everyone has different levels of expectations and that's okay. What we all have in common is life, a life that is worth living. We deserve to be happy and happy with the amazing little families that we've created. I was lucky, I had lots of support, but I am under no illusion that it is not the same for every mummy.

From the ashes of my postnatal depression, *Sentient* has been born. Sentient means 'to feel', it's a safe place to talk, seek help and have a helping hand in making steps forward in a positive way. I work with Neuro-Linguistic Programming and Creative Art Therapy with many other mums around the world. I can help you too. Learn how to build an anxiety tool kit of your very own, one that you can use whenever you need it and fast. *Sentient* runs group programs and one-to-one support coaching. Together, I can help you identify your triggers and help you to form your path forward out of the darkness. NLP empowers you to live the kind of life you want and wish to create. You hold that power; you can do anything you want. It's all about mindset and changing those limiting beliefs. Keeping things simple and manageable, yet moving you forward in a positive way, with big fat huge steps! You can start such changes today; it's that simple. As an anxious person, simplicity is key. If you feel overwhelmed and pressured, you're not going to commit to or want to stick to anything. It's all about language and blocks. Change the language, your outlook, lead from within and boom, magical things start to change in your mood and everyday living.

You see, NLP allows you to shift, no medication needed, and it sticks with you for life at an unconscious level. It allows you to take control of your thoughts and behaviour. It's a brand-new attitude and, as an anxious person, one that is gold for getting out of the slump and fear. NLP is a huge personal development tool. It's your life…be the driver of your own bus, not a passenger! You can create the life you want to live, and you don't need money to do it. Don't let labels, the stigma of a mum role or other people's expectations define your day. Do what makes YOU happy, taking full responsibility for your actions and behaviour is empowering. This is a huge part of NLP. I don't only use NLP to make big changes either. Journalling and getting creative can also help you to instantly reduce your anxious feelings. Switch off a messy head and keep your hands busy. All this, I can help you with and it works. Let me be your guide to moving forward, not back. I've been there, it sucks; I can relate to your words for sure (even the scary ones that you don't want to say out loud). You're not alone and it's OK to not be OK. What isn't OK is living life for years on end in this slump, in darkness and pure loneliness.

I am also here to tell you that you've got this and that you are doing a fab job. Life as a mummy is not easy, and certainly not easy when trying to battle postnatal depression. However, if you don't make the change, then everything will stay the same. If you're not moving forward in any way, then you will stay in that moment or even in the past. Just spend a minute and say the following to yourself…

You are a one-off creation, you, never to be repeated.

There is not one other the same as you anywhere on the planet.

Compare this to the material world, how valuable would you be?

How much do you think a one-off Ferrari would be?!

You are worth a fortune and irreplaceable.

With the right support and tools for change, the sun will come back out, and you will enjoy those muddy, giggly days with your family again… I Do!

Want to know more?

Get in touch for a big fat brew and a chat. You can find me on Facebook: www.facebook.com/nikki.sawyertofeel   or join my group www.facebook.com/groups/feartofreedomformums a safe place to reach out and tons of support from other mums feeling very similar to yourself, tortured by anxiety and low self-esteem. From me to you there are also freebies to access within this group that can help you start to make the shift needed in your mindset today, dump the mum guilt, live free from fear and be the driver of your own bus.

You can also visit my websitewww.niklasawyer.co.uk and get in touch for advice to aid change, support and friendship there too!

You're not alone, I am here, and I've been where you are now xxx

About the Author

Nikki Sawyer is the founder of Sentient. She is a Life Coach and Personal Development Mentor, a mum of three and a full-time Entrepreneur. For the last two years, she has supported and helped many mums all over the world to find their own identity and reduce their anxiety. Coming from a dark place herself, Nikki shares her journey and relates to many other mums and the daily challenges and tough moments life can bring.

Website: www.nikkisawyer.co.uk
Facebook: www.facebook.com/groups/feartofreedomformums
Email: niklasawyer@outlook.com

Transforming Pain to Gain: Rising From the Ashes and Unleashing the Best of You

By Dr. Julienne Dizon Shin, PhD

The Pains

'Maybe I deserved it'.

As I sat on the curb with this very familiar thought, in the dark, with tears down my face and blood dripping from my mouth. I was so taken aback about why another incident like this happened over something that I never knew would be a source of conflict in my personal life.

I was twenty years old, newly married to a man I thought I knew. As the arguments escalated into physical fights, I kept telling myself that it was just this one time. I also was conflicted with feelings of being stuck in a bad place and that 'this must be normal'.

I left home at seventeen years old to join the Marine Corps, not because it was a longtime dream of mine, but because it was a way to escape the violent place that I was supposed to call home. Boot camp was a breeze for me because I recognized it was for intense training purposes, acculturation and no physical or verbal abuse would compare to where I came from.

I soon realized I had an odd sense of attachment to home and actually missed my family. Later I would understand that this was just part of the loss I felt of not having a healthy functioning family. I would come home when I could and it suddenly felt that I had earned the right to be loved because it wasn't the same. But then again, I knew I could leave and wouldn't be around long.

As the only female most of the time, I revelled in the attention I was getting from the male environment. It felt like I was filling a hole inside my heart. But these quickly evolved into heartaches and regret. One late night a senior ranking Marine firmly stated that he needed to do an inspection on my room because I had missed one earlier that day. As a Marine, I was taught not to defy orders and had a sense of intimidation of authority, so I did as I was told.

That night, he decided that he also had the authority to also take my body the way he wanted. Despite my weak efforts of saying no and I was not comfortable, he did as he wanted and I was raped. I immediately went into a play dead mode and disassociated as I had always done during moments of intense fear as a child in the face of violence and abuse. I did not identify it as rape, but as something I had brought on to myself. I felt guilt and shame because I might have enjoyed it and did not fight back more aggressively. But mostly because I felt that *maybe I deserved it.*

I soon found out I was pregnant, and it devastated me. More so because I was so ashamed, scared and felt so alone. I did not have any close friends and I knew I could not turn to my parents. This would shame them. I felt so flawed, used, broken. After weeks of deep depression and intense fear, not knowing what to do or how to handle it, I had an abortion. I went alone and scared. I left afterwards even more alone and even more scared, ashamed, and guilty. But, as I had been trained to do, I moved forward and did my job the best way I could as a Marine.

I feared being 'found out' so much that I focused on being in top physical shape, being proficient at my job, and getting promoted. I kept up with the male Marines in physical fitness and the long arduous military combat hikes and received a commendation for my work. I became one of the 'boys'. While inside I felt unworthy, a fraud, and lonely.

When I found that one 'nice' guy and he talked about marriage, it just made sense because, why not? He was the sweetest guy I met since I had joined and did and said small things to defend me and 'care' for me. All the others always seemed to be only after sex. Following my incident with rape and abortion, I was vulnerable, and a little bit of kindness felt like I had found treasure. I thought I had finally found someone who truly loved me. Little did I know

I did not know what love was because I never experienced it and I did not even love myself.

When his first act of anger came at me, it surprised me, but I also quickly reverted back to the 'play dead' and dissociation mechanisms, not fighting back. I felt the fear that I had been accustomed to as a child overwhelm me.

A turning point in my mindset came after a heated debate about religion caused him to punch me and I ran outside. I'm not sure if it was to run away from him or to find help, but he did not follow me. I sat exhausted and not knowing where to go and repeating the same narrative of 'maybe I deserved it'. After trying to wrap my head around why it had even got to this point, I decided the only place I could go right then was back inside. As I was tending to my wounds in the bathroom and wondering if I could use makeup to cover up the inevitable bruising that would appear the following day, he came in and brought roses and a bottle of pills. I cautiously looked at the roses and with a confused look picked up the bottle and saw it was Motrin. He said with a regretful tone that he was sorry and hoped these would help.

He thankfully left me alone and I knew right then that this had to stop here. The deep anger welled up inside me as I looked at the 'gifts'. Even in my state and after years of abuse, I knew this was not 'normal' and essentially, was fucked up. Who brings roses and Motrin after beating up a woman? No. this needed to stop and no man was going to do this to me again.

My life did not immediately make a change for the better after this moment. It took time, courage, and direction. It also took gaining confidence through physical strength and effectiveness in defending myself. Kickboxing and weightlifting helped me to recognize the physical strength that I can have and feel more confident.

After focusing on what I did not have all my life to empower me and pull me out of a mindset of fear, I changed direction and focused on ways to help others. I became an avid community volunteer and soon an international volunteer. Through these experiences, I saw through the lens of those with different cultural backgrounds and values, those with different kinds of challenges and pains. But also, those that so admirably found joy and peace in the simplest things and the most austere environments. I envied them as I saw the way they navigated the difficult life they were given. Little did I know that despite their lack of basic needs or even a war around them, they had strong families, love, and safety that gave them a different mindset to survive. Something I was not familiar with as a child.

I also realized I never had anyone that looked like me to emulate and learn from. So, I chose to pursue the leadership side and become an officer where I would be able to make more of an impact and be an example for other young ladies following behind. This path as an officer lent its own challenges; as I faced a male-dominated organization as a minority female leader at the table, contending with racism, oppression, continued misogyny, and frustration from being discouraged to have a voice. All the things I experienced as a child of immigrant parents in an all-white world being repeated. But this time, I was taking action. Going to fight a war I did not fully agree with and leading young adults with similar opinions who were nervous and unsure only added more unique challenges; witnessing the worst violence humans can do to each other, collateral damage suffered by women and children, psychological and moral damage.

My life journey contains similar other stories that have knocked me down, beat me up, and dragged me through the mud. What did I have that kept me going? I constantly felt I had to prove myself because of my low self-worth, loneliness because I had no one I could turn to, severe depression, and an underlying sense of always being wrong or not good enough. I felt a constant sense of fear of being in trouble for something, even though I never did anything wrong. I was a consistent hot, tangled mess inside that did anything to keep it hidden.

The ironic answer is that the abuse, fear, and shame kept me going. I grew up with the belief that no one should see anything bad that is happening with our personal lives. We should always put on a strong face and keep our mouths shut. And this is what I did. I looked great on the outside, I performed what was expected or more. But I would fall apart when I left work. No one knew the secret I carried of a deep depression that would fall upon me as I went home alone and struggled with the demons inside me. Watch television for hours and sometimes drink a bottle or two of wine till I went to sleep. Or passed out. I made up for this by excelling as much as I could as a Marine, take college courses to try and 'find my way', or pursue grand endeavors that might make me more 'worthy'. Even after twenty-four years of successful military service, commendations, awards, and a PhD, I still struggled with what 'worthy' meant.

The Gains

The pains I experienced became a source of strength throughout my lifetime. However, little did I realize this nor did it always manifest in a healthy way. I survived. And that is what the pains did for me. Survive. It took decades before I was able to see how my pains became my gains and make me the person I am today. I am thankful for each and every trauma and the goodness that it has put in front of me. Now I am able to truly connect, resonate, understand and help others, especially when I found the peace and acceptance that my heart, mind, and soul were searching for in order to function as a fully healthy, happy, and whole human being.

But how does this 'pain to gain' concept look? As human beings with unique differences, this obviously looks different with each person. However, the main three pains that resulted in various experiences are underlying common basic emotions that can drive people's behaviors. There are numerous other 'pains' that are associated with traumatic events in life that can manifest other gains, but for the purpose of this chapter, I will reflect upon how the basic three became a driver to powerful gains in my own personal life.

Fear. My experience of a violent childhood instilled much fear early in life that persisted through this abusive marriage and even through many years of a successful career. The gains I learned from this was learning the reality was that fear can be a source of good things too. I learned to question why I feel fear and if it is a real or perceived fear? What's the worst that can happen? Most of the time, as an adult, it was nothing. Other times, my fear was telling me something not right was happening and I needed to take action. Fear helped me find my voice at the table. Fear helped to identify injustice and take action. And now, as I work with clients and patients, I have a sincere understanding of the fears they have that are obstacles in their life.

Love. The absence of love and sense of safety in a child's life truly has an impact on self-worth and value. Relationships were difficult. Friendships were difficult. Sex was complicated. Career was difficult. I didn't understand why and thought it was normal until I realized years later that none of it had to be THAT difficult and it was NOT normal. The gain I learned from this painful experience was being able to personally understand how much feeling worthy, valued, and simply enough influences our lives in nearly every way. No matter how successful or happy one may appear to the world.

Anger. My experiences of an abusive marriage, violent childhood racism, discrimination, oppression from having a voice, misogyny, witnessing injustice and unnecessary losses in combat, and the women and children who were collateral damage not surprisingly made me an angry human being. Coming home after a war and feeling as if the world was more worried about money and material goods infuriated me and I wanted to disappear. The gains I later learned from these painful times was how this emotion is like fear. It can push or prod someone to be destructive...or effective. Since in much of my life I did not realize what was happening inside my psyche, I was mostly destructive to myself. But as I learned to harness that anger and understand it better, it was one of the biggest drivers to making a change. I sought out ways to be a better leader than those I had seen. I chose to further my knowledge and education so I could be more of a resource for others and improve the way I could be in this world with others. I took action on injustices that I saw happening around me to others or myself.

Emotions are a sign from your body that should be attended to and listened to. They are neither good nor bad if we see are able to see them as simply symptoms of something that needs attention in our bodies. I like to call them my alarm system.

One of the most helpful tools I learned to use was self-awareness, paying attention to my internal world; what was I feeling, why was I feeling it, what kind of conversation was I having with myself on a daily basis, were these feelings and conversations valid and why they were even present? Be cautious when talking with yourself because YOU are listening. If your inner child is broken and not nurtured or healed, any negative conversations with yourself will continue to be the pain throughout your life that keeps you from being happy, finding peace, and feeling your self-worth. Just as it did for me. 'Maybe I deserved it' was the common theme I held in my head for years every time something bad happened and I attributed it to my own self-worth. Once I pulled myself out of that and changed the conversation to, *I don't deserve this, I AM worth it, and I DO deserve good things*, I was able to move forward. Again, this is not an overnight process, but took years of self-reflection, further learning experiences, choosing the right people who supported me, and being able to talk to people I could trust.

All of these experiences have helped me to be a better psychologist and coach as I resonate deeply with what I hear, the emotional, mental, and physical obstacles that keep people from growing and coming into their own. I am able to be a better collaborator and guide in finding their strength and together we find the one true road that leads them to it.

As a friend, lover, mother, daughter, these experiences have helped me to be more aware of how my actions and words can easily help or hurt those I choose to be in my world. And yes, I have learned to CHOOSE who is in my world. Those who make me feel nothing less than who I am, those who give me nothing less than authenticity. Those who encourage and lift me and who allow me to do the same for them.

For my clients and patients, and to better illustrate the

transformation of painful experiences into something better, I use the visual of a rising phoenix to reflect the empowerment of this process. Furthermore, the ashes from which I came is not forgotten but accepted and loved as part of the person whom I am proud of today. I would not be here without these ashes I have risen from. I do not let my past define me, but become a better part of me. Once your mind and heart embrace this, life looks different. And peace from within is found.

You may not know me. Yet. But I see you. I hear you. I feel you. Because I've been there. Deep sorrow, deep anger, deep hurt, massive frustration, no sense of value, no sense of direction. Deep depression and doubt.

Life can feel so HARD. But it doesn't have to be. It took me longer than it should have been to learn this. However, I also learned to appreciate the adversity I've experienced in my life because I am who I am today because of BOTH the good and bad. My mission elevated from keeping the nation safe to helping the people IN the nation find personal safety, love, happiness, joy, and direction. It is a purpose I have more passion for than I ever realized as I feel the immense joy of each person's growth, no matter how small or large it may be. I may have found my own way in life, which has been the best accomplishment I could have reached. But that accomplishment becomes even more meaningful and lasting when I see how my past pains are able to become the significant gains of those I am honored to serve.

About the Author

Dr. Julienne Shin is first and foremost a proud mama. Julienne served twenty-four years in the Marine Corps with two combat tours, which led to her transferring to the Navy as a Psychologist. She realized through her sexual and combat trauma, harassment, misogyny, racism, and oppression throughout the years, just how critical it was to be resilient with a growth mindset in order to move forward and succeed. She found that the same strategies were critical for her consecutive careers, life, as well as being a mama in order not to get bogged down by setbacks or stuck in negative thinking.

Now as the Mindset Cure Doc, Julienne proudly serves as a Coaching Psychologist, passionately sharing her experience through coaching fellow entrepreneurs and business owners from being stuck, overwhelmed, stressed, anxious, or depressed to having clarity, success, and momentum in both their business and lives.

Website: www.drjulienneshin.com
Facebook: www.facebook.com/julienne.shin
Email: info@drjulienneshin.com

Why School Screws Us Up - And How We Can Fix It

By Ellie Jayne Baker

Introduction

Have you ever wondered if school is screwing up your children?

It's a fear that gnaws away at me on an almost daily basis. In the UK, where my family and I are based, we're fortunate enough to have our kids in a 'really nice' primary school, where subjects like music, arts and languages actually still have some kudos. However, the story across the rest of the country couldn't be more different.

My ten-year school-teaching career really opened my eyes to the narrowness of the education system, and I became increasingly frustrated by the very essence of it. I could see the damage it was causing young people, but like so many teachers I felt completely powerless to effect any change. We were bound by pointless and destructive policies and systems imposed by autocratic institutions that were completely out of touch with young people, which served only to boost the image of the school in the eyes of the public. Our hands were tied; and while we played the hoop-jumping game, both teachers and pupils suffered.

My subject, languages, underwent huge marginalisation thanks to this system which favoured 'core subjects' like English, maths and science. While so much of the world seemed to have the right idea, starting children learning a second or even third language before they even started school, our kids were forced to wait until age eleven, missing out on the most crucial language-learning window of opportunity (0-7 years) completely.

While I was saddened by this, I shouldn't have been surprised. My own school years had taught me that I was a bit of a 'freak' for loving languages so much. As a white girl born to English-speaking Welsh parents, you could say I was in the minority to have a passion for languages and other cultures from such a young age. Growing up in a predominantly white working-class town in the Midlands, to say that there was an absence of cultural diversity would be an understatement.

We left Wales to settle in Worcestershire when I was five, so I was forced to learn quite early on how to adapt to a different culture. It may be easy to assume that there are no real differences between the Welsh and English ways of 'being'; (though I dare you to say that to a Welsh person)! However, despite being so young and 'adaptable' I distinctly remember the sense of loss and grief I felt for the sing-song familiarity of the Welsh accent, words like 'cwtch' and the endearing overuse of words like 'lovely', 'babes' and 'ooh there's han'some ewe are' (handsome wasn't an adjective uniquely reserved for boys, which I think made Welsh people rather progressive even in the eighties)!

My re-education into speaking 'properly' was well underway just two weeks into my new school life. By the summer of that first year, I was almost fluent in 'Brummy' and I would forevermore be teased by our Welsh counterparts for being posh (yes - posh)!

I guess in some relative ways, we were a bit posh. Unlike so many of my school mates (and all of our Welsh relatives), by the age of six we had already visited France a good handful of times, and the summer holidays soon became something to look forward to for more than just a break from school.

My curiosity for this new culture and language peaked at around age nine when I met a French girl of the same age at the pool at our campsite in Normandy. Both families connected for the duration of the holiday, and a relationship began which still continues more than thirty years later. I finally had a motivation to learn this fascinating language that my dad seemed so at ease with. I was determined to acquire this superpower too, so when I started middle school the following month, I was ecstatic to learn that French formed part of the curriculum. I could never quite understand why almost none of my classmates felt the same way. Why did they groan when it was time to get their French books out? Why did they find it so innocuous, when I found it so meaningful? Needless to say, I threw myself in with gusto.

Losing My Love of Learning

The school years rolled by in a flurry of numbers, spellings, awful gym pants, angles, Tudors, playtimes, hard times, friendships, bullying, awkwardness, ties, blazers, boredom, essays, grades, demoralising lectures about UCAS, fear, parties, apathy and a crushing sense of pointlessness.

At the end of it all, I just felt lost. I was bright, and a deep thinker. But I messed up my A levels and I couldn't figure out when things had started to go wrong. The innocent enthusiasm for learning that marked my early years seemed to have drained out of me slowly after my first year of middle school, like a sneaky puncture that I never even knew was there.

The little girl who was so wide-eyed, 'so clever,' so full of potential had been squashed, muted, numbed by the enormity of the expectations of the education system. Her love of French was still there, but it was buried under the stress, anxiety and confusion of everything else. She felt rebellious, angry, and apathetic all at the same time. All she did know was that she loved how she felt when she was speaking French or daydreaming about visiting faraway places and trying new things, learning about other cultures and immersing herself in infinite possibility. Surely, there were so many ways to do things! Was there really only one 'right' way to live? Couldn't you just choose & create your own future? Why were these adults treating us like lemmings, scooping us into this funnel in the hope that most of us would come out with 'acceptable' letters and numbers stamped on our foreheads? Wasn't it all just so dull, so predictable, so inhuman? Was this all there was to look forward to?

For a while, I watched in stunned confusion as my friends scurried around, terrified, doing one of two things; applying for university, or trying to get out of school and into employment as soon as they could. You either knuckled down to the system or did all you could to avoid being a part of it. I wasn't in the latter camp, but the former seemed pretty terrifying too.

It wasn't until it dawned on me that soon I'd be left alone while my friends disappeared and started new lives, that I finally took action. I scraped together the few points I had from my A levels and, in true 'Sliding Doors' fashion, made it into university by the skin of my teeth.

Reigniting the Fire

Once the party season of the first year was over, I got into a rhythm and found that my fire for language learning was fully rekindled. With Spanish thrown into the mix, it was certainly a challenge, but after years of feeling lost and wasted, it was a welcome one.

Mixing with other linguists was refreshing, exhilarating,

empowering and liberating. My feelings of apathy towards my former studies were finally normalised and understood. We were explorers of humanity, in search of anything that threw our own culture into question. We were philosophers, historians, political activists and freedom fighters; ready to break through the walls that British society had built around us.

The third year loomed large for us - it was the 'year abroad'. Waiting to find out where we would be placed was as agonising as it was exciting; we knew we had little control. It was a total lottery. When the letter finally arrived, I remember my hands trembling so much that I dropped the envelope twice! It felt more momentous than anything I had ever experienced before.

Finally, in September 2000, the plane touched down in Marseille's international airport. It felt like everything I had ever done had led to this. Strapped for cash, I lugged my oversized, impractical thirty-kilogram suitcase to the station and onto the TGV platform, before nearly dislocating my shoulder as I dragged it all the way to the school lodgings where I would be living for the next seven months.

With its white tiled floors and hospital-style decor, it felt so stark, so cold, so unfamiliar. My nerves were jangled; after a long journey, I was wired. I missed my mum, my boyfriend, and my best friend who was just ninety kilometres away in Aix-en-Provence. What had I done? Why didn't I just stick with the route that everyone else had gone down? At least then I wouldn't be facing this gut-wrenching experience. As I tossed and turned on my new plastic mattress that night, I started to realise just how far outside of my comfort zone I really was. And I didn't know if I had the emotional resilience to deal with it.

The next day I presented myself, sleep-deprived but with my eager face on, to the Directeur of the secondary school where I was placed in Avignon. I was charged with teaching English to groups of fifteen pupils. I'd had part-time jobs before and wasn't work-shy but this felt so formal, so scary! Some of the 'kids' I'd be teaching were only a few months short of my mere twenty years. 'It'll be fine', I told myself, 'they will be so enthralled with my native English! I'll be like a local celebrity in no time'.

Well, this couldn't have been further from the truth! My naivety and inexperience were soon sniffed out by both the younger and the older kids; most of my classes were riotous. I soon learned that the school was dealing with a number of challenges, including demoralised staff who saw language assistants, such as I, as an opportunity to take a cigarette break. Alongside this ongoing battle and lack of support at the school, over the coming months, I would face a number of challenges and life-changing experiences that would shape me forever.

The Transformation

The infamous and brutal mistral wind finally began to subside in February, which meant (admittedly, with some relief) that it was time for me to say goodbye to Avignon. It had been a rocky road; I'd dealt with an attempted mugging, being robbed of my purse and phone on a train, being flashed at while in a phone booth at night and being stalked by strange men on an almost daily basis. I'd lived in two flats; the better one I'd stuck with despite the terrifying 'night fights' that regularly took place outside, the crunching of blood-stained glass beneath my feet as I braved yet another walk to the school that didn't really care if I showed up or not, and trying to make peace with the mould and cockroaches who were so determined to be my flatmates.

I'd made some lifelong friends, made awesome progress with my French and had travelled to some wonderful places visiting friends who were placed around France and Switzerland. I'd grown in confidence; I was more assertive, more determined. But I was weary and ready to move on.

I needed to call time on my Avignon adventure, which was meant to last until April. I knew if I could get out of there in February, I'd stand a chance at getting into a Spanish university for the second semester. No longer afraid to question authority, I made my case to my university and lo and behold, my prayers were answered. "Can you leave in the next week?" asked the powers that be. Er... YES!

The memory of lugging that thirty-kilo case onto the bus, and then sitting on the back seat, watching Avignon grow smaller and smaller until it was almost nothing, will be forever etched into my memory. It was cathartic, euphoric, even. I had very little Spanish under my belt really, and my head was so entrenched in the French language that when I tried to tune in to the frequency of the gabbling Spaniards on the bus, I was shocked to discover I could barely understand a word. 'Here I go again', I thought to myself. I could have been terrified, should have been terrified. But no, not this time. It felt electrifying. I realised, in that moment, that my old self had gone. I wasn't the same Ellie that arrived in Marseille five months ago. It felt like a lifetime had passed since then. Avignon had seemed like a trial of endurance at times, but I knew it had been a test. And I had passed, I'd won the prize; Salamanca here we come. For the first time in my young adult life, I felt totally and utterly free.

The Realisation

Our final year back at Clifton Campus began like no other. The seventy-odd young adults that sat in the lecture hall were the same as those awkward, slightly immature twenty-year-olds I'd sat with just fifteen months before; but yet they weren't.

I realised there and then that our experiences stood us apart from our peers. We were wiser, more enlightened. There was an unspoken understanding; a level of respect for each other that dissolved any past assumptions, disputes or pecking order that existed between us before. Studying languages had opened doors into a new realm, a new dimension of self. In choosing this path, we'd inadvertently embarked on a journey of introspection, forced to face our demons, to get to know the deepest, darkest depth of ourselves. By challenging our own cultural norms and beliefs, we had gone through what some refer to as 'the dark night of the soul' and we'd come through the other side, transformed. This cultural agility that we had developed within ourselves was the real treasure.

Determined to share this realisation with the world, I dived headfirst into my language teaching career, where I spent ten turbulent years fighting with the system. Every day felt like walking a tightrope as I tried to keep up the fight to keep language-learning alive, while simultaneously trying not to get buried under the strain of what was a flawed, broken system.

Unwilling to choose between a questionable, draining career and motherhood, the birth of my daughter saw me close the door on the classroom. Determined to give my daughter a better start in her formative years, and to bring her up with a sense of awe and humility for the world, I embarked on my quest to make language learning mainstream in the UK. I realised as I looked into my baby's innocent little squinty eyes that this was a monumental task that couldn't be tackled top-down. It had to start at the ground up, at grassroots level. With the birth of my baby, the seed of an idea, 'BilinguaSing,' was born too.

The Solution: The Creation of BilinguaSing

Up until this point, I had worked with children and young adults ranging from four to eighteen, but now, suddenly, I had a precious little baby in the world. I truly believe that a language is one of the most precious gifts you can give a child; the younger we can start teaching them, the more adaptable and capable their little minds become, instilling a love and seemingly natural flair for languages all the way through their life.

I started a small 'Spanish through music' class with my own little girl and a group of local mums. I had no idea how it would grow and develop, but it just felt like the natural thing to do. We had so much fun as I used this group to develop what is now a unique, sensory music class with a second language at its heart. What surprised me most was the high demand.

Parents of small children recognised the value of this new type of class and saw their attendance as more than just a morning out of the house, but an investment in their child's future. Soon I was running multiple classes in multiple languages every week, welcoming children aged 0–5 years to different sessions and being invited into nurseries and later even primary schools.

The best part was the difference these classes were making to children and parents. I wanted to do more, but I physically didn't have the capacity; I simply couldn't meet the demand on my own. This was when I decided to franchise the business. I had created a class that was unique and so valuable to my own community. I had done all the hard work creating music, content and a brand that was now bigger than just me and I was ready to share it with the world. When I took on my first four pilot franchisees, I was terrified; but after seeing their success, I knew it was right, and I could see the potential for further growth. Watching more and more families be inspired by language learning, with parents re-writing their stories of being terrible at languages at school and finding a new zest for life felt like nothing else!

BilinguaSing had become more than I could have imagined. It might not have been my original dream as a little girl, but my classroom teaching career gave me the best foundation to build an even better one.

The Future

So here we are in 2021, in the throes of a pandemic which has (aside from everything else) disrupted education in so many ways. As a nation we had already set ourselves adrift from the rest of the world by choosing a new path outside of the European Union; our little and not-so-little ones blissfully unaware of what this could mean for them. Recent world events have held a mirror up to some of the most brutal sides of humanity: inequality, xenophobia and ethnocentrism to name a few, further widening the already gaping chasm we need to cross to repair the damage and start to heal. In short, we have a long way to go. But where there is education, there is hope.

When we teach children languages, we allow them to think openly, to be curious about other countries, their people and to be part of a global community. By giving young children the opportunity to become culturally agile, we broaden their horizons. In doing so, we can begin to rebuild the fractured world we live in, gluing it together slowly, piece by piece, country by country; making us the whole that we were always meant to be.

We can start to fix the shortcomings of our education system when we realise that it's actually far less about the languages themselves, it's about the riches we uncover beyond them. A second language gives you the keys to the castle; it's what's behind the locked door that changes everything. To the point where it feels unimaginable to me to have got this far in life without ever having unlocked that door. To the point where I feel sad for those who have had this truth hidden from them and therefore have been unable to hunt for the keys. There is more than one way to live, there is more than one 'right', there is more than one 'normal'. Once you know this truth, everything that once made sense to you before no longer does make sense. You question yourself, you question your culture, your upbringing, and whether the country that raised you is where you really belong.

I get that this can be scary. We fight against it, we resist, then we grow. As a result, our lives become richer. We are happier, more open, more empathic, more human. Isn't that what life should be, a journey of continual enquiry, curiosity and a bringing together of humanity?

Imagine a world where we focus more on what unites us, and what makes us all human? A world where we relish learning new things from each other? Why not embrace it, and allow these lessons to fill us with joy and wonder, replacing the hatred and fear?

Isn't that the world we want our children to inherit?

Quite simply, I believe our children deserve the best opportunities in our complex and divided world. We have a duty to start this 'world healing' process on their behalf, and in doing so we show them the way forward and equip them with the tools and skills they need to continue this overwhelming task, which our generation will sadly not be around to complete.

We can't ignore the impact that COVID & Brexit are having (and will continue to have) on the decisions we make about what young people actually need to thrive today. By teaching our children languages, we can mitigate the impact of these events and offer this and future generations the best chance of a brilliant future; one full of joy, opportunity and limitless potential.

If this speaks to you, I'd love you to join our growing tribe of parents, educators and language-lovers who, together, are helping put language learning firmly on the map. Together, we are creating a movement that calls for a total overhaul of our education system, putting intercultural empathy at the heart of it.

United, we can reboot both world relations AND education from the ground up.

About the Author

After three years teaching English as a foreign language and a short stint in the corporate world, **Ellie Jayne Baker** qualified with a PGCE in French and Spanish in 2004. During her ten-year teaching career, she worked in a variety of secondary, middle and primary schools in numerous roles, including head of subject and teacher trainer.

When her first child was just five months old, she quit the classroom to set up her award-winning children's language & music class company, BilinguaSing, which she franchised in 2014. BilinguaSing offers a fresh and stress-free approach to teaching and learning languages, having helped thousands of children and their families learn languages through her unique musical approach.

Today Ellie is a pioneer for change in education. She coaches teachers, writes about education and helps her network of BilinguaSing franchisees to thrive in their businesses. She's an 'extroverted introvert' who dreams of living a nomadic life, educating her kids while travelling the world; but for now, lives happily in sunny Maidenhead, UK.

Website: www.bilinguasing.com

www.elliebakereducation.com/blog

Facebook Group:

www.facebook.com/groups/BilinguaSingFamily

Email: ellie@bilinguasing.com

Dream Like a Child: How Living in Partnership Connects us to Dreams, Action and Magic

By Sarah Beale

We all have dreams when we're kids. Sometimes they're outrageous. We want to be princesses or movie stars, have unicorns as pets, live in an ice cream factory, invent cars that fly. My kids don't necessarily have outlandish dreams but they don't limit themselves to just *one* thing that they might want to BE. My youngest, during a game of 'best friends' (she plays it with me and we're, well, best friends) worked in Starbucks, cut down trees, mowed lawns and drove a taxi. My oldest wants to be an actress and a zoologist. My boys are already living their dream life! Why wait?

Being called a 'dreamer' has long been associated with not having a firm grip on reality; of being separated from what's possible; of not being grounded on what can actually be done. Dreamers are impractical, fantastical, romantic beings. When attached to the female form, the connotations place dreamers in the realm of the insane.

But consider this: a dreamer is one who is concerned with what is *possible*; what *might* be; what is achievable if only one could let go of the limitations of other people's opinions and the restrictive nature of what *is*. What *must* be.

I always felt like a dreamer but the words of others ringing my ears, 'not everything can be fun, you can't always enjoy what you do', and the desire for financial independence, saw me take a run of fun, but certainly not ambitious or visionary, jobs. These jobs were in shops, bars, restaurants and finally, for a government agency. They were all service-based and very much rooted in tasks and productivity. I tried to improve every place that I worked; often meeting resistance and assurances that 'we do things this way for a reason'. I even worked with a woman once who was insistent about the way we kept pens on the desk. But I've always had this sense that things could be different and so persevered. Or quit. I possibly had a bit of a reputation as a quitter and it's something that has stayed with me until recently. But what it is, is that I enjoy things that have their basis in *how things could be*. And that doesn't mean I can't enjoy things NOW - quite the opposite. It does mean that I can visualise how things might be and anchor myself in that; feel it almost and then, with a combination of magic and movement, make my way there.

It's one thing to dream, right? We all daydream about tropical beaches and exotic holidays (or, in my case, camping, dirt and cooking on a fire) and imagine, when we allow ourselves the luxury, how things might be. But what is the difference between someone who settles for the occasional daydream and someone who *turns the dream into* REALITY?

As in all things, it's my children who have shown me.

I believe that children are born dreamers. If they weren't, how would they ever have the confidence to take their first steps; climb the slide the wrong way; launch themselves from high places? Children think not about what could go wrong, they think only of what might go right. To the programmed eye of a parent, this looks like risk-taking but kids see it as living.

A young child, maybe below the age of six or seven, lives out much of their life in an in-between world of dreams and fancies. Part imagination, part reality. To them, their dreams are truly real. The small child walking down the street with an imaginary dog can actually see the dog. Is it real? Of course. But adults have mostly forgotten how to dream and can't see it. Is the child dressed as Captain America, really Captain America? Sure. Only an adult would try to ground the child in reality by insisting they take their outfit off for bed, the supermarket or school.

My children all lived deeply in their dreams for several years (one or two of them are still there); there was my oldest daughter who had two imaginary friends from the time she could talk. We could tell they were very real for her. She also had a passion for Alice in Wonderland and seemed to really believe she WAS Alice. I believed her. One of my boys was deeply into Teenage Mutant Ninja Turtles and would spot all the manhole covers in the street, expecting Mikey or Leo to jump out at any moment. Sometimes they did.

But something happens to many children some time in their first decade of life, to make them question their 'mind world' (as one of my children calls it). It might be a parent or other adult telling them to 'stop being silly' or to 'stop pretending'. It might be school where kids are expected to spend the majority of their day steeped in the adult agenda. We're told that it's a natural evolution into 'real life', but I wonder...imagine what it must feel like for a child, living between worlds, to be told that one of those worlds isn't real. Might our world be just teeming with dreamers if we allowed children as many years of inhabiting this in-between place as possible; if we didn't force them into scheduled activity, pre-school and school, would they stay in that place much longer, dreaming their impossible dreams, living fully in their hearts?

So how do dreams make it beyond the 'dreaming' stage? And does it matter if they do? I think there's a place for both, but I prefer to sit in the space where dreams become reality and that requires a commitment to change and ACTION.

Dreams + Action = Change!

Because kids really are not limited by fear, practicalities, logistics, limiting beliefs etcetera, they easily move from dream to action. A child unconstrained by timetables and adult agenda will wake up every day with an idea of what their day might be like. It naturally includes no such thought as 'I won't be able to do this' or 'xyz might not work out'. They get out of bed with a sense of anticipation and wonder of what the day will bring; this state of mind seems to allow them easy and almost instant access to, whatever they want! They dream it, they DO it.

What makes it so damn hard for adults to access this childlike sense of *knowing*? Did someone tell us during our childhood to stop playing; stop talking nonsense and be sensible; stop getting distracted and get your work done; you can't wear your princess outfit to the shops; stop being lazy and be productive?

Without a dream, we can't make any internally driven changes and our lives will be determined by the agenda of others. Parents expectations; societies expectations; peer pressure.

Somewhere between blanket forts, endless loads of washing and preparing snack plates, I forgot how to dream. This story is, at its heart, about the gift my children have given me in not only being completely themselves but reminding me how to dream; how to turn my dreams into action.

When I stopped working to be with my first child, I approached my days with familiar purpose. Familiar because it's how I'd approached life for some years. I wasn't some kind of super-efficient robot with endless to-do lists and lots of ticks, but I certainly congratulated myself at the end of a day with all that had been accomplished. This surely was the way to happiness, right? Or at least the sort of satisfaction that allows one to be rewarded with meals out and the odd pair of new (Italian) shoes. Work hard. Feel the reward. And so without paid work to fill my days, I simply filled them with unpaid work. Same, same. I continued producing children and approached each new life with the extra allocation of jobs requiring my time. I enjoyed my children of course and I even, for years, convinced myself that I enjoyed folding nappies, making banana bread and folding clothes. But all that busyness leaves little time for dreaming. With endless tasks stretching ahead, imagining anything different seems pointless.

My soul tried to nudge me though, and I made holiday plans, organised birthday parties and threw myself into Christmas celebrations; this stuff was fun, sure, but didn't fulfil me in the way I felt it should have. What I was discovering was that plans do not equal dreams. And without dreams, well, there's no change. By the time my fourth child was weaned, I was in a rut.

I felt it, I knew it. I dreaded getting out of bed to attend to the sameness of the day. Make breakfast, pack lunch boxes, get kids up and ready for school. Any school mums reading this will resonate with the drudgery that is finding shoes, wrangling kids into school jumpers and the worst thing - dragging them away from playing lego/animals/drawing/playdough/painting the walls, to go somewhere they didn't really want to go. Well, mine didn't anyway. The essence of living the life of your dreams is questioning all of the *shoulds* placed on us by society and if I needed more evidence that my kids lived fully in their dreams, it was their resistance to school. It's often described as a symptom of a disorder (or at the very least a personality quirk): School Resistance. It's an actual term, denoted by capital letters I believe. I've wondered, particularly since mine stopped going to school, what stops parents from seeing it for what it really is: a child insisting that life holds something more for them than someone else's agenda and an instinct to turn away from things that control. Creativity cannot be harnessed and I think children know this.

I'm so grateful to my kids for always being who they are, no apologies, and pushing me into a place of radical acceptance of them. When we left the school system several years ago, we knew that we were embarking on a great adventure; a journey of lifelong learning and a commitment to living together in a different way. So much possibility when the school hours are freed up and there is no schedule to stick to. So much space is created. Space for dreaming. Space for those dreams to transform into action.

With the limitations of timetables and external structures removed, our family was really able to dig into how *we* wanted to live. How *we* wanted to relate to each other. I realised just how stifling school had been. There was no longer a need to wake the kids up which translated into later bedtimes. Dinner could naturally run later as the kids stopped regularly bathing in the evening - personal care can happen at any time of the day you know. A midday bath? Why not? Or *gasp* no baths! And the best thing is that each child was able to invest their time in whatever they felt drawn to; no limits; no timeframes; no arbitrary curriculum. I realised too, that without any external structures forced on us and less need to eat in a certain way or to wear specific clothes, I had some time to spend any way that I wanted! I could finish a thought, read a book, sit down to drink my coffee and, you got it - DREAM. I started small. I imagined the day ahead of me - a luxury that hadn't been afforded me for some years (the great oxymoron of parenting small children is that it's so consuming there's barely a chance to look beyond the task one is engaged in NOW, and yet one is also pushed to administrate school forms, dentist appointments, drama costumes and playdates). But then I started to think about the big stuff like what kind of life we really wanted and how we could further free ourselves from what I was feeling more and more, were the constraints of modern urban life.

I remember my husband confusedly asking me, 'What more do you want'? We had a great house in a lovely neighbourhood; we were financially secure and had a fabulous community around us. It's true that on paper we looked like we had everything we could want. And yet, yes, I did want more. More purpose, more abundance, more joy. What did that mean exactly? Well, we were to find out! Unschooling was just the start.

Living in flow, for this is exactly what was happening once space was created for MORE, showed me what could be possible when we hand our dreams over to the universe and take steps to materialise them. During a three-week separation, thanks to a US work trip for my husband and a road trip up through Queensland, Australia, for the kids and I, a plan was hatched. We would sell our home and most of our belongings and set off on an adventure.

A couple of years later and we are still on our adventure - it's taken a weird and slightly sci-fi turn, as have all post-2019 adventures!

The real story is what happens for our children when they are free to be completely themselves and how, with our trust transferred from a school system that doesn't serve us, to our children, the magic of being human thrives.

I observed my children in infancy and as young people and saw that they were capable of a great deal without my assistance - they rejected it actually, quite determined to learn how to crawl, babble their first pre-verbal sounds, put food to their mouths and later, more complex tasks like dress themselves and cut vegetables with me as I prepared dinner. That toddler declaration of 'I DO IT' is confidence indeed and not misplaced because, based on mothering for thirteen years, I see first-hand that they can! There are very real reasons why parents are tempted to interfere with a child's natural learning process: fear that a child won't be able to manage a risky situation, scheduling that makes it difficult to allow for thirty minutes to put on a t-shirt, expectations of how a task should be done. Sometimes we just think we know better - because we're grownups. Consider this though: by interfering with a child's innate ability to try new things and their confidence in their own ability, we inhibit their desire to try, and put the weight of our own fears and limiting thoughts on their shoulders. Often, by the time they've even reached school age they've not only forgotten how to dream but they've forgotten how to take risks and try new things.

A child who lives without limits, on their time or their personhood, operates quite differently to a child who is controlled by schedules and the agenda of others. They have almost endless time with which to not only perfect tasks and activities that are important to them but can direct their energy as they wish. Delving deeply into a passion, spending time with it as a friend and not an adversary to conquer, allows for an intimate knowledge unlimited curriculum. It's less likely that kids will break up knowledge areas into subjects, instead extending learning naturally to the whole realm. A passion for Marvel Comics naturally includes history and myth, science, language and relationships. A child playing with trains will build, count, learn about motion and probably role play. As a child gets older, they may naturally want to learn to cook and will refer to books, the internet, select recipes, shop for ingredients and prepare the food, incorporating reading, maths, science, problem-solving and art. And being able to engage with their interests in an unhurried manner will further encourage them to become immersed in the process and not the outcome - another distinction of children who are free to learn in their own way and an important bridge to dreaming and activation later in life.

When a child is not performing for results, awards or recognition, they are more likely to learn for the sheer joy and become engrossed in the process rather than how things will look at the other end. Less attachment to a specific result allows for pleasure in the journey, wherever that may lead. One of my earliest memories of what I now see as natural human behaviour is of my oldest daughter as a three or four-year-old and her dedication to her crafts. She would sit at the dining table for hours and fiddle about with plasticine and sticks, glue and glitter and make the most wonderful creations. She rarely showed me; instead, I would find them when guests for dinner necessitated the cleaning of the table. I marvelled even then that she would spend so much time and dedicate such attention to her art for nothing more than the joy in the doing. While other children are coerced into producing specific projects for stars on sticker charts or certificates for spelling tests, a child living without school will be free to commit to an activity - or not. With no fear of punishment of repercussion and this opens up a whole world of creativity and dreaming.

One of the common concerns of parents considering a life outside of the school system, and even more commonly, presented by parents who are more comfortable living within the paradigm of control, is, 'how will kids learn how to follow rules and how will they learn things like how to treat others and manners?'

Living without rules or agenda presents children (and grown-ups) much opportunity to feel the weight of their own autonomy and the impact they have on others. Not by being explicitly taught how, but by feeling it and practising in their own way. In our family, this philosophy of personal freedom was very much demanded by the kids. In that conventional 'top-down' model of parenting, a child questioning a grownup, saying 'no' or challenging requests or rules is most often not tolerated. The parent, believing that acquiescing to these sorts of challenges will result in constant rule-bending, lack of respect and maybe outright mutiny, seeks to control. Better not to let it get started! But in a family where everything is up for negotiation, nothing is off limits, beautiful opportunities for connection present themselves almost constantly. Instead of shutting a child down with a principled 'no', a child might be invited into a conversation about why and what might be possible. And almost anything is! Which not only opens up all sorts of creative ideas but it sets a child up to be empowered, to own their own life and to learn, quite naturally, how to take responsibility for it. Which includes the impact that they have on others, organically and when it's appropriate, with divine timing. Consider: a small child is supposed to put themselves first - they live in their ego and really don't start to notice how they relate to others until six or seven. A child demanding a pink cup when you've offered blue or a toddler drawing on the wall when really we'd rather they use paper isn't challenging us because they are being naughty or trying to test limits. They are doing what comes quite naturally - exactly what they want! That's not to say that a child younger than six won't be able to learn about relationships and their place in a family, and actually many children display very early signs of empathy, just that there's no need to force or to explicitly teach a child how to relate to others, or the world. How could they not; they're human after all and to be human is to seek community and all the comforts that a village provides. It's in their nature to fit in, to be accepted. Like other animals, children learn how interconnected we are by observing and interacting with others. Without imposed rules and arbitrary limits, their sovereignty can develop over time, as do their relationships to others - but not before the most important relationship. To self.

The biggest realisation I have experienced since becoming a mother, and here is the paradigm shift, is that children are born whole; not as empty vessels to be filled with our knowledge. Just as humans have raised ourselves above other animals, to achieve sovereignty *over* other species, we have, as adults, elevated ourselves above children. Sure, some wisdom comes with life experience and practicality suggests that there are things that grownups need to guide (my kids can't drive a car for example so I'm kinda in charge of transportation!) but kids can be responsible for so much more than we give them credit for. And they hold their own unique wisdom as beings who are often far more connected to self than we are.

Since leaning into how I see my kids naturally learn, naturally just *are*, I've noticed my own confidence for trying things out, returning to me. I remember it from when I myself was a child - it wasn't gone after all, only lost for a while. This desire to give things a go, whatever the outcome. The letting go of attachments to how things will work out and what they will look like. The freedom to push myself without fear of failure, judgement from others and the subsequent shame that can arise when we forge our identity on how others see us. And most of all, the alignment that finds us when we let go of control and live in our dreams is where the shifts happen. The change. Like magic.

A child who is free to learn and free to BE is naturally more, well, *them*. The parent of one of these children enjoys that same freedom as a birthright.

About the Author

Sarah Beale is many things. Only one of them is a mother. She is also a collector of kitsch knitwear; a sourdough addict; a bird whisperer (her daughter doesn't believe her); a late-night Netflix viewer and a somewhat regretful border collie owner (she wanted a lurcher). Her children have brought out not only the very best of her but her most real self, the self that shows up authentically, lives joyfully, walks barefoot and sings loudly. It is in that spirit that she co-founded The Partnership Parenting Movement and seeks to bring that same sense of connection and playfulness to other families. She supports parents in undertaking the inner work required to live in freedom with their children and advocates for self-directed learning and life without school and runs group programs that help others live in freedom.

Sarah is a writer and a thinker and has recently contributed to other soul-aligned projects. You can find her blogging about all the things rattling around in her brain at www.radicalthinkingradicalliving.com.

Website: www.partnershipparent.com
Facebook:
www.facebook.com/groups/thepartnershipparentingmovement

Healing the Wounds of Capitalism and the Patriarchy

By Laura Niehorster

I glanced at the sun setting outside the Victorian windows; it had been a beautiful day. I had been living it vicariously, watching the photos of my friends sunbathing in the park pop up all afternoon on Facebook. The lights in the university art studios had been slowly switching off as students and teachers gradually left to go enjoy the last of the warm weather. Eventually, my small corner of the studio was the last one lit and the pen scratching in my notebook echoed around the empty room. There was no one to hear my stomach rumble or tell me to go home as I rubbed my sunken, sleep deprived eyes. This particular memory was from my Art Foundation Year, but during my entire education I missed out on a lot more: cocktail day drinking, poker games, beach trips, nights out, chip shop outings and countless other socialising opportunities which I'd never be able to get back. I thought this was the best way to live my life.

As someone who's very sensitive, intense and feeds off external validation, I learnt what the rules of our society were at a young age and internalised them in order to be successful according to our western society. Academic and professional achievements were the only ways I knew to measure my success; I wasn't aware you could measure it in terms of family, relationships, health, happiness or life experiences.

Capitalism is the economic system most of our world was built on, where profit is prioritised.

Capitalism teaches us to work until it's uncomfortable.

That pain is progress.

Hard work will bring us happiness.

That we must earn rest.

That we need to make sacrifices to be successful.

And I epitomised this.

My headaches started when I was a teenager. They meant I woke up every morning in pain and went through the day battling a cloud of suffering to focus on my schoolwork. The pain and extra effort taken to ignore it and keep working was so draining that I didn't have energy left over to socialise or have fun. They made it hard to concentrate, talk and read. I was taking painkillers most days which occasionally had an effect. The solution provided by our medical system was to provide me with stronger drugs, which also barely worked.

I learnt to push through in order to keep functioning like everyone else. I embodied the toxic masculine qualities our patriarchal society promoted: being strong and aggressive - pushing to keep going and be the best, hyper independence and glorifying unhealthy habits. Our patriarchal society is based on the belief that men are superior to women and should have power over them. The pain in my teenage body was trying to tell me that I was overwhelmed and I should be kinder to myself and slow down, but I had learnt to disconnect and ignore my body as a coping mechanism and as part of the masculine belief that intellect and logic are more important than what we feel.

After graduating from university, I tried to start a business making machine washable sanitary pads, to help the environment and potentially help those experiencing period poverty. The idea tapped into the conversations which were happening at the time and quickly gained momentum locally. I did a TEDx talk, basically my first public speaking experience. I put so much pressure on it to create the perfect talk, like my idols and veteran writers and speakers Brene Brown and Liz Gilbert. I became part of a business accelerator, where I won a competition to pitch to investors from New York. I was one of the winners of a nationwide British government competition looking for young innovators who wanted to improve society. The more support and achievements I gained, the more pressure I felt to make the company a success.

When I started my company, I also started doing a lot of self-development work to learn how to be a better leader and entrepreneur. I joined a group called Simply Sisterhood to network with other female entrepreneurs and at the time, their spirituality and feminine energy had freaked me out as it was so alien to me and it was what society had taught me to judge. Over time, I opened my mind to their teachings but I struggled to practise them after internalising decades of patriarchal and capitalist values.

I went to Bali for a month with my boyfriend in summer, a trip that was meant to be a month in a tropical paradise to relax together. I also wanted to use the power of this spiritual mecca to go inward. On the first day we were finally alone, I awakened in the middle of the night throwing up. The next few days were spent between the bed and the bathroom, hiding in the AC, stuck in a crowded tourist city while the paradise I'd been desperate for waited miles away. I reached out for help to my spiritual friends and they told me that throwing up was my body's way of purging. They told me to let go of the things that weren't serving me.

I managed to get up enough strength to move to a beautiful house in the countryside of Bali, but my stomach muscles and body were so weak, I had to spend the remaining two weeks of our holiday recovering from my illness.

Toxic masculinity is disconnected from and doesn't value nature. It values logical, predictable and consistent machines over soft and cyclical nature; just look how the patriarchy has treated the environment. Mother Nature is a powerful representation of feminine energy: she creates, heals and nurtures all life on Earth. Like women, she is subjugated by men for profit and power.

Nature reminds us to slow down. Nature takes patience: nurturing a plant requires regular care and seasons of love. The peaceful rice field paradise was almost mind-numbingly slow and quiet at times. But there was something therapeutic about being able to observe the passage of time through nature, the original clock, before everything was calculated down to the millisecond. Being able to watch the sun travel through the sky and darken as it sets from the same spot was probably my most healing experience of the holiday.

Being forced to stop gave me time to step back and analyse myself and the society I was part of, whose values I'd internalised.

Slowness is in contrast to our society which idolises busy.

Slowing down is going against the system and will feel unnatural, like swimming upstream.

For months after, I was still healing from the realisations and experiences I'd had during that trip. I went to Bali to have a spiritual experience, thinking it would be graceful and beautiful. Instead, it was dark, messy and scary. To this day, I don't even know what happened or how I'd explain it to others; it felt like a high functioning implosion. All the layers of me had been peeled away and what remained was a small, weak, sensitive baby. My identity had been wrapped around the masculine qualities of being strong and independent and constantly making progress. The house that made up my identity had been knocked down and so many of the bricks had been washed away, I didn't know what I had left to rebuild with.

While I was trying to recover from my spiritual awakening, pressure was mounting in my business. I had prepared financial projections and an investment pitch and flew to Belfast for an intense few days at a business conference pitching to investors. I was also packing a bag and prepping meals to stay at a friend's house in a different city every week so that I could be part of the achievement focussed, aggressive business accelerator programme. Although these days were exciting and the community invigorated me, they were draining and took me away from my relationship which was also falling apart. The stress was compounded by my headaches, which made every day feel like a battle. Going through daily activities was exhausting and felt like wading through mud. I had to put on a front to the outside world in order to function and in private, I could barely function once I took the mask off. I was torn between my business and relationship and ultimately decided that I couldn't handle either in my current physical state. I broke up with both in the first few months of the new year.

I spent winter and the start of spring in hibernation, following the patterns of nature. I embraced the feminine energy which the Simply Sisterhood had been teaching me about all along. I had the mental space and time to surrender to rest and give my body what it needed. My life was now much simpler, having intentionally dismantled all the pieces which held it together. I started getting alternative treatments for my headaches which felt more nurturing and empowering than the drug-based, ten-minute consultations I had had with GPs.

I learnt to be kind to myself. All of myself. My headaches had taken so much from me and I resented them; they were disempowering and debilitating. Grieving the things that chronic illness has taken is completely valid, but I was sick of feeling like a victim. Spending that time quietly getting to know myself again helped me accept my health conditions. I used to blame my headaches for all the "bad" things about me: being tired all the time, having dark thoughts easily, being highly strung. I used to think I'd be happy when I got rid of my headaches.

But what if I accepted them and worked with them, rather than against them?

What if I lovingly accepted that I need more rest than other people and can't plan too much into my day?

What if I stopped judging myself for my dark thoughts and being highly strung, and talked to myself compassionately?

I used my new feminine skills to embrace my feelings. After my last breakup, I had fought my pain and emotions, not being able to accept them. This time, I trusted the process, *feeling* what was right instead of thinking. I knew it was okay to hurt and to let myself feel everything that comes up without judgement. I knew I could be strong and still hurt, and that I'd come out of it a better person. I trusted myself and my instincts, knowing they were guiding me in the right direction. I didn't rush forward to be over him or feel better, just let myself grieve.

After months of hibernating, I booked on to a meditation retreat. It sounded terrifying but powerful: ten days in complete silence, no contact with the outside world and no media to distract us: no books, TV or even pen and paper. Just meditating all day, every day. The solitude of the retreat put a really strong emphasis on everyone having their own journey and being responsible for themselves; no one's going to tell you what to do. So, I had to rely completely on myself. Every time I was down, the only person who could bring me back up was me, so I learnt to use my feminine skills to nurture and trust myself. The process helped me to really know in my heart what everyone had been telling me all along: that all the answers I needed were inside me. I got to learn who I am at my core: stripping away all the conditioning, social cues, influences from the media and outside world. I learned who the real me was: not the dark, crazy, scary version of me who I'd been terrified of and had been fighting to push down, but a positive, relaxed, problem-solving woman brimming with self-belief and strength. I learned that I can't be "fixed." I can't find out the one big thing that had been wrong with me all that time, the thing that had been causing all my problems, and dig it out with a knife. It was going to be lots of little steps and take time, love and patience.

I started dating again for the first time in six years. When I'd started dating my ex, I was so scared of getting hurt I hadn't opened up or let him into my heart, I'd barely enjoyed the honeymoon period at the start of our relationship. This time, I embraced my feminine energy, started dating with an open heart and surrendered to whatever came up. It was scary; we were both intense, sensitive people who got emotionally involved quickly. It was intoxicating and I lost myself a bit, losing my footing in my world and getting pulled into his. But I let go further and trusted the process, reminding myself how much strength I'd gained during my hibernation. Really feeling alive again with someone new was exciting, and *hot*. I got to connect with my sensuality in a different way than I had before: as an adult who was responsible for my own pleasure and confident in her sexuality. I experienced kink for the first time with him; experimenting with submission with someone who I trusted, who prioritised my pleasure and cared deeply about me was so freeing.

I want to give in to you.

Release.

Let everything go.

I want you to take it from me.

Forcefully.

Persuade me to give it to you.

Take me to the edge so that I can't hold on any longer and my grip releases.

Take it, it's yours.

Then I was able to learn another lesson in embracing my feminine energy: flexibility, listening to my gut and going with the flow. I'd healed so much at the beginning of the year but I started feeling held back by the stability and impatient; ready to open up and have new experiences. I booked my first solo trip after seeing a TV show about the creative, liberal city of Austin, Texas. I embarked to a city I knew nothing about with no plan, only the first few nights in the hostel booked.

For the past six months, I'd been living a quiet, simple life and spending lots of time by myself. In Austin, I met a group of psytrance DJs who partied every night in a warehouse they'd brought as a collective. I ended up hanging out with them most days and getting back to my hostel at the time I'd have been waking up back home. I made no plans for my entire trip but every day was a new experience with the types of people I'd never met at home. I found my home and my family in Austin. My new friends were adventurous, working on exciting projects, creative, loved to party and liked me for who I was. Austin was a creative, colourful and loud city: around every corner, there was new street art or a performer, an innovative street food stall or a lovely creek walk. Leaving after ten days was a heavy bump back down to reality and forced me to surrender further.

Do you become desensitised to heartbreak after having to let so many beautiful people go?

Or do you accept that love and spiritual connections flow in and out of your life, trusting that the right ones are coming and you're ready to receive the love you need?

I'd always loved plans; they made me feel secure, like I was on a safe path and knew where I was going. I'd often stuck to them to my detriment, no matter how unhappy or unhealthy they made me. I'd get lost in the plan. I was overwhelmed by the complete shift in what I wanted and my identity; I hadn't expected to find so much joy in connection, unpredictability and intensity after the simplicity of my life back home. My instincts told me I had so much more to do in Austin; my small, quiet life back home now felt so restrictive and like I wasn't able to live up to my full potential. I wrenched out my plan for the future and reevaluated, vowing to return to Austin for longer.

I felt guided to continue living like I had in Austin, but this new way of living felt scary and I didn't know if I was strong enough. The changes would take me away from the safe, structured healing and to something a lot less predictable. It felt like the ground was moving underneath me, but I trusted it would open up to reveal something new and incredible. Life sped up and I realised I wasn't scared of the darkness anymore: it was exciting.

I'm searching for something intangible, something ephemeral.
It's a feeling.
It's an experience.
I think I'll find it at the edge.
I want to go to the peak, maybe I'll find it there.

It's not just one thing, one "aha" moment.

It's a body of work.

I won't know when it happens, only once it's happened.

It'll come from chaos, not discipline.

It'll come from darkness, not light.

I'll find it when I'm lost.

I'll find it past the boundaries of my old life.

I need to jump the fence, leave the warmth and glow and wander out into the darkness.

I'll find it in the unknown.

I first learnt about edge work reading Fear and Loathing in Las Vegas. It put a name to what I'd been doing after I returned from Austin and made it real. According to sociologist Stephen Lyng, "edgework explores the world of voluntary risk-taking, investigating the seductive nature of pursuing peril and teasing out the boundaries between legal and criminal behaviour; conscious and unconscious acts; sanity and insanity; acceptable risk and stupidity."

Before I went to Austin, my masculine values had made me always want to be in control.

When I returned, all I wanted was to find new ways to let go of control.

I wanted to see what happened when I let go of the wheel.

Feel the rush of adrenaline

When the panic sets in.

Because it was new and I didn't know what the outcome would be. Unsure whether the risk was worth it.

Without my Austin friends and a new exciting place to explore, I used my instincts to follow what felt good, finding new ways to challenge myself and make life exciting back home. I used the approach I had in Austin and went to an art bar, started talking to people who looked fun and ended up making friends with a group of creative hippies who loved to party, just like I had in Austin. To break up the long weeks in the office, I challenged myself with more extreme activities in nature. I started swimming in the freezing British sea before work; the cold water helped my chronic pain and the adrenaline hit made me feel alive and strong. I went on micro-adventures on Tuesday nights: leaving the office at 4pm, driving out to the countryside and walking into the forest or on to the cliffs with a backpack where I'd cook myself noodles for dinner, sleep in a bivvy with the night breeze on my face and layers of stars above me, packing up in the morning and getting to the office for 10am on Wednesday, my colleagues none the wiser where I'd spent the night.

My life was on a pendulum swinging between chaos and the discombobulated, floating feeling, with the resting place between them being peace. On these nights by myself, with just the sounds of the waves crashing over the rocks as I watched the sun set with my noodles, I felt at peace. Giving up my business, breaking up with my boyfriend and everything else I let go of brought me so much peace.

Peace is something I'd always strived for but didn't realise. But you can't fight for peace. I always threw myself into things head-first, chose the hardest route and aimed higher than I knew I could achieve. But what I really wanted all along was to be at peace with myself, at peace with my life and my choices.

What if I didn't need to prove myself and always be achieving to know I was worthy?

What if I could be at peace with myself as I am?

My peace levels vary now: I know it's always there, but sometimes I have to wait for the rough waves to subside.

In the new year, I made it back to Austin and I worked in the same hostel where I had felt instantly at home last summer. The hostel experience was intense: it was a small, sociable hostel where the guests loved to party. It was impossible to have quiet time by myself, I was always surrounded by people, there was always something fun and exciting happening and I never got to bed before midnight. It was perfect.

I also joined the Austin kink community very briefly and got to experience kink outside of a romantic and sexual partnership. Shibari is the Japanese art of rope bondage. It is one of the most intense, spiritual, cathartic, physical and connected things I've done. As someone being tied and a recovering control freak, it was so powerful to have no choice but to let go. Fighting for control would have made the experience much less enjoyable.

I let go and I was constrained, but I felt free and strong.

Giving in to the rigger and trusting them with my mind and body. I experienced how much my body could endure and push my limits.

My mind was focussed and meditative.

With all of the physical sensations happening, there was no space to think, only feel and be present.

It was healing.
It was emotional.
It was therapeutic.

It is hard to turn a complex, messy lived experience into a short narrative that neatly flows from one point to another and there is a lot that I left out from the last few years for the sake of conciseness and privacy. I reclaimed the feminine energy which I'd learned to suppress during my youth and connected with the sensuality I'd never really embodied as an insecure young woman, made to feel ashamed of my body and sexuality by our patriarchal society. Neither energy is inherently bad or good, both masculine and feminine need to be balanced within everyone, regardless of our gender. But myself and many others in our patriarchal, capitalist society have become disconnected from our feminine energy because society has taught us those qualities are weak and should be subjugated. If you'd like to come on this journey with me to regain your own balance, you can follow me on Instagram @radical.sensuality or join my free Facebook group, the Radically

Sensual Femmes to reclaim your body, sensuality & feminine energy. The group is a safe space to unlearn and gain freedom from the harmful lessons that our patriarchal, capitalist society has taught us. We are releasing shame, learning to express ourselves freely and enjoying our sensuality.

About the Author

Laura Niehorster is a fashion design graduate who expresses her creativity in many ways: textiles, painting, writing and self-portraits to name just a few. She has had many creative projects over the years including pursuing fine art textiles, an enterprise creating machine washable sanitary pads (an environmentally friendly alternative to disposables) and now sensuality coaching with her business, Radical Sensuality. The underlying quality which unites all of her projects is an admiration for women's strength and a desire to lift them up. She is fascinated by society and understanding how it works; her analytical brain enjoys researching and dissecting to discover the social values we're subconsciously perpetuating. Laura is an adventurer whose most powerful memories of her travels are of the people she met along the way and stories they told her; she is honoured to gain insights into the lives of those who are different to hers.

Instagram: www.instagram.com/radical.sensuality
Facebook Group: www.facebook.com/groups/radicalsenses

Workplace Wellbeing: More Than Just a Checklist

By Phoebe Jackson

I am on a mission to change the way workplaces approach and manage the wellbeing of their employees!

The events of this year have shown us all that changes can be made when circumstances force a change. I believe that we should be considering different, more effective ways of working to bring about positive change, rather than doing so because we have been forced to by a worldwide pandemic. In general, humans are creatures of habit and will continue on a certain path because it is what they are used to or because that is what others do. They do what society expects. Why keep doing something in the same way, just because that is what has always been done? Why not be innovative and radical and find ways that things can be done more effectively? Work is such a huge part of many people's lives and can have a significant impact on the other areas of their life. This is why it is so important to make it as positive an experience as possible.

Certain events in my life have led me to this point. My personal life and my work life have often intertwined and I have had both positive and negative experiences. My journey to this point began around five years ago when the father of my son passed away suddenly on Christmas Eve. That was the worst day of my life and something I still struggle with to this day.

I was due to go to work that day. I called my colleague and told him what had happened. My team were incredibly supportive and I am so thankful that I had such wonderful people around me to help me through such a difficult time. Unfortunately, HR was not as supportive and this is where my understanding of the importance of wellbeing in the workplace began to develop. I was told that because I was not in a relationship with my son's father at the time, I was not entitled to take any time as compassionate leave because he was not on the approved list of relatives. It didn't matter that I had a four-year-old son who was grieving for his father and needed his mummy with him or that I was struggling with my own feelings of loss, he wasn't on the list so it didn't count. I found this way of approaching the situation completely bizarre and inhumane. This is one of the hardest things I have had to deal with and at a time when I needed time to grieve and to comfort my son, I was given the added financial worry due to having to take unpaid leave. Now, I understand that policies have to be made and lines have to be drawn but what shocked me was the lack of flexibility and the inability to see me as an individual, with a unique set of circumstances. If I had lost a relative, it wouldn't have mattered how close I was to them or what the impact was, I would have been given compassionate leave.

I've known stress in the workplace. I've worked with murderers in prison and been the centre of communication for a well-known theme park and handled ride breakdowns, accidents and missing children. Working in a psychiatric hospital, I've seen people in extreme distress and listened to horrific life stories. I've helped patients who have wanted to end their life and been hit and kicked by them when I have stopped them from doing so. As a social worker, I've been threatened, spat at, and verbally abused. I've been bitten by a dog during a visit and I wrapped my arm up and still drove my service user an hour to her hospital appointment, asking a nurse to patch me up when I got there! I've witnessed severe deprivation and worked with children who have been abused, neglected, and lost their parents. I have enough stories to fill a book of their own! All of this causes a certain kind of stress, but with positives to balance it out, it can be managed and I did manage it for several years. The thing that pushed me over the edge was stressful situations, with a lack of support to balance it out.

Social work is a notoriously stressful career, particularly the area of child protection. I began my social work career working within an extremely busy child protection team in a deprived city. Caseloads were high and resources were scarce. I found this job extremely stressful at times, but I had a supportive team and manager which made it manageable. Whilst working in this role, my mum became unwell with anxiety and had to be hospitalised.

My dad suffers with Parkinson's disease and I am an only child. I am also a single parent and this meant that I had a lot of people relying on me, with a lack of support. This cocktail of stress brought me close to breaking point, I continued working and trying to juggle my various commitments whilst descending into a pit of stress and anxiety. Luckily, I had a manager that knew me, that had shown a genuine interest in my life and realised that there was something wrong. She wanted to help and support me to continue working, rather than putting me under further pressure. She changed my working hours so that I was able to drop off and pick my son up from school twice a week, which made a massive difference and significantly reduced my 'mum guilt'. She asked how I was and told me that my family was my priority. If I needed to answer the phone to my mum's nurse or nip up to the hospital to drop things off, this was not an issue. She praised my work and showed me that I was valued as a team member.

As time went on and my mum was able to go home, things settled down. A job opening came up at a local authority in my local area. I decided to apply as my commute would be much shorter and more pleasant and the caseloads were much lower. At the interview, I made it clear that I would need flexible working and that if this was not acceptable, they should not offer me the job. They offered me the job and assured me that I would be able to continue with my current working arrangements. I was torn. Did I want to stay in a supportive team, with a supportive manager but with a high caseload and a commute that involved sitting in traffic for around an hour? Or did I want to take a risk and move to a team in a better location with a reduced caseload, but with a team and manager that I didn't know? I took the risk and accepted the position, which turned out to be one huge mistake!

From my very first day, I got the vibe that this was not a great place to work. There were some nice members of the team who were welcoming and supportive but others gossiped behind each other's backs and put others down to make themselves look better. The manager fuelled this by joining in with the gossiping as well as patronising and micro-managing team members. She also had the attitude that if you are not working sixty-hour weeks and constantly sacrificing your personal life, you are not a real social worker. She made me feel like I was incompetent and useless, despite that fact that I got my work done and by her own admission, to a good standard. There were comments like, 'I'd better ring them, you won't know how to handle it', and to my senior colleague who had checked a court statement for me, 'Is what Phoebe's written a load of crap?' Then things progressed. One afternoon, she called and asked me to do a non-emergency visit to a person who was not on my caseload and who lived an hour and a half away. I explained that I did not have anybody to pick my son up from school and I wouldn't be back in time, but that my colleague was happy to swap tasks so that I could still finish on time. She replied, 'No, I want YOU to do it', and insisted that I would be back in time. I told her she was arguing with Google Maps, not me but she wouldn't listen and shouted at me until I put the phone down.

The situation peaked when my mum became unwell again. I was

having supervision with my manager when my mum's nurse called to tell me that she was having to be hospitalised again. Obviously, this was upsetting and worrying for me and I became emotional. My manager's response to this was, 'I can smother your mum with a pillow for you if you like?' Then she turned to her computer and started answering emails while I sat there trying to process what had just been said. She then joked that I could have my son accommodated into care to take some pressure off. I just could not understand how someone could be so devoid of empathy. This was the turning point for me. I went home. I went to the doctors and I was signed off sick. This was the first time I had ever had to be signed off sick and it didn't feel good. I had the smaller caseload, the nicer commute, but the lack of support meant that I just couldn't keep myself afloat any longer. I felt pathetic.

Following this, I wallowed in self-pity and worried about how I would ever return to work. I attended counselling with a wonderful counsellor who helped me come to the realisation that the way I had been treated was unacceptable and that I needed to make a change. This manager had been from team to team and had had similar complaints made about her but instead of senior managers dealing with this, they just moved her to another team. I decided I didn't want to work for an organisation that allowed bullying to go on unchallenged and I handed my notice in. They had ticked all the boxes in terms of wellbeing provision, but this just didn't translate. They had an employee helpline, counselling sessions, physiotherapy sessions, and team "away days" but none of these things helped me to stay in my job. When it came to employee wellbeing, they talked the talk but didn't walk the walk.

This was a major turning point for me. I felt like something should be done. I had seen so many colleagues and friends leave their job roles due to similar issues and it seemed completely avoidable, with solutions based in common sense. I thought about how this can be the case for so many people. People generally have to fit their lives around work, rather than the other way round. I reflected on my own experiences and decided to do some research to see if my ideas about how things can be improved had merit. I completed surveys and interviews and found common themes, confirming my own assumptions and beliefs. I looked into employee sickness statistics and found that in the UK in 2019/20, stress, depression or anxiety accounted for fifty-one percent of all work-related ill health cases and fifty-five percent of all working days lost due to work-related ill health. When the statistics are so high, why are employers not doing more to address this? Possibly because they don't know how to? Possibly because of the cost of seeking advice or implementing a wellbeing strategy? However, as the statistics above show, it costs a lot more to not address it. A wellbeing strategy should be individual to each business, company or organisation and the needs of its employees; there are steps that every employer can take to improve wellbeing. My education and experience in mental health, psychology and social work, combined with my personal experiences places me in a unique position to help.

Firstly, prevention is better than the cure. It's good to have

employee helplines, mental health first aiders an
but it is better to build a culture where pec
listened to and valued. My experiences and r
to develop the TRACK model. This model incorpora
most important factors in building a wellbeing strategy. Tru
Relationships. Adaptability. Communication. Kindness.

Trust

Trust is absolutely vital in creating a positive culture and it is reciprocal. The easiest way to get somebody to trust you is to trust them. When workers feel trusted and in turn, trust their employer, they feel more settled and confident in their role, leading to higher productivity. If workers do not feel trusted, this can lead to worry, stress and anxiety about constantly evidencing that they are doing what they are supposed to be doing. This means they are distracted and spend time focussing on less important tasks to "seem busy". Micromanaging does not work. It causes stress and drives good workers away. If somebody is not fulfilling their role as they should, this can be identified, investigated and dealt with appropriately. In my experience, good workers will work hard without needing to be constantly monitored and not so good workers will find ways around any monitoring.

Relationships

Building positive relationships creates a positive environment and benefits everyone. It means that people are more likely to be open about the challenges they are facing and not allow it to build and p into a greater problem. Treating people with respect, king them and acknowledging good work helps them to feel alued. There should be time for having a chat and having fun. Many of the respondents in my research identified their relationships with colleagues as an important factor in combatting stress.

Managers cannot always solve the problem that an employee has, particularly if it involves their personal life. However, they can help by acknowledging the issue, listening and having empathy with the person and considering ways they could improve the person's work life. Treating people as individuals, taking a genuine interest in their lives helps a manager to understand how to get the best out of people and to spot when something may be wrong. Being assertive and knowing when and how to say no are vital in maintaining positive relationships.

Adaptability

As we have recently found out, businesses need to be adaptable and flexible to survive and thrive. This could include offering remote working, offering different shift patterns, part-time hours, freelance work. Valuing output over working hours could also be beneficial. Various studies have shown that people are more productive when working less hours.

In terms of my own lifestyle and preferences, remote working has improved my wellbeing and there are many personal, financial and societal benefits to companies working in this way as much as possible. On a personal level, people will save time and money through not having to commute. I used to spend two hours a day in my car, in traffic, getting frustrated and impatient. This equates to around twenty days over a year! I now get to spend more time with my son and work when I feel most productive rather than during set office hours. I can take my dogs for a walk in the middle of the day or take some time out on a hobby.

Remote working enables people to work from anywhere, meaning that people can live outside cities but still work for traditionally city-based companies or even travel the world as long as you have an internet connection. This also enables companies to source talent from anywhere, increasing diversity and equality of opportunity. The costs of renting or buying office space are drastically reduced. As we have seen throughout the COVID-19 pandemic, there are also benefits to the environment due to the reduction in commuting.

However, there are also many considerations for wellbeing when remote working. Blurring work and home life can be an issue, particularly if you are not disciplined about your working hours. There can be distractions; children, pets, deliveries etcetera, however offices can also be distracting places. I've known people sit and chat in an office for hours at a time and have meetings for meetings' sake.

When working remotely, employees can lack connection with other team members, particularly those who are new to the team. To avoid this, workplaces should maintain regular communication via check-ins, supervision, virtual "elevenses", in-person meet-ups, retreats or conferences. These types of events could also be adapted to be more relaxed and inclusive. For example, bringing children along, no dress code and choosing different locations or settings based on what the employees prefer.

If employees don't have a proper set-up in terms of equipment, this can cause strain injuries or issues with reliability of tech. Equipment should be provided and set up in the same way it would be in an office environment.

Communication

Communication is key in any business or organisation, regardless of if they are worrying about wellbeing or not, and if done right it will certainly help wellbeing. During my research, respondents identified improved communication as the most important thing in improving wellbeing at work. This was closely followed by training in mental health, resilience and managing stress. It is important for people to have clear roles and responsibilities and to understand what is expected of them. Likewise, if they are struggling or do not understand something, it is important for them to raise it. Active listening helps the listener to fully understand the situation and respond with empathy and possible solutions. It can also help to diffuse situations and achieve compromise. This links back to having positive relationships. Training is important in conveying the company's values and helping expand employees' skill base and progress.

Effective communication can also make change easier. People can often struggle with change, particularly if it is unexpected. I can recall a time when I was informed that my job role had changed significantly via email on the date that the change came into effect, which was extremely disconcerting for me and my team. Where possible, consultations should take place and as a minimum, employees should be well prepared and know what to expect.

Kindness

This is relevant to everyday life, not just work. Treating people with kindness costs nothing and could make a huge difference. You never know what somebody is going through in private. In the workplace, people should be treated as a human being with a unique set of circumstances, not just a number. It can be as simple as saying thank you, asking how someone is, or acknowledging good work. Research has found that feeling valued and appreciated at work can lead to better physical and mental health, as well as increased motivation, engagement and job satisfaction.

The way a manager or workplace responds to a worker in crisis can make the difference between them staying in work or going off sick, staying with the company or leaving, recommending them as a place to work or warning people to stay away. Ask how people are and mean it. It can be difficult to know how to respond when someone is upset, particularly if you do not know them well. This is where training for managers can be extremely beneficial.

What I've learnt from my work history is that it's not always the most stressful job or situation that causes you the most stress. It is more about the balance between positive and negative; a high caseload but a supportive manager, an emergency situation with a supportive team, a long day with a thank you at the end of it. I truly believe that when it comes to work stress, the smallest things can make the biggest difference. Effective communication means more to people than beanbags in the office or the odd 'away day'. Yes, these things can help but if you show people they are valued and appreciated on a daily basis it will have a much more profound effect.

When the COVID-19 restrictions are gone, it will be good to have some things return to normal, but when it comes to the way we work, let's be innovative, flexible and forward-thinking. We shouldn't have to sacrifice our lives for work, work should be organised around our lives.

About the Author

Phoebe Jackson is a Workforce Wellbeing Consultant. She has had a long career working with vulnerable people and supporting people to make changes in their lives. As a lone parent, she is passionate about work-life balance and after living through personal challenges, she understands the importance of looking after wellbeing. Phoebe helps HR directors increase productivity and reduce staff sickness, presenteeism and staff turnover; by providing a bespoke consultation service, her innovative TRACK method helps companies develop an effective wellbeing strategy. Also passionate about the environment, Phoebe believes that addressing employee wellbeing by using forward-thinking and innovative solutions, companies can also reduce their carbon footprint.

Facebook Page: www.linkedin.com/in/phoebe-jackson-a466b41b7
Facebook Group: www.facebook.com/groups/868640977005711
Email: phoebe@yourworkforcewellbeing.com

From Overweight Office Prison to Dream Body Opportunities

By Jen Harrap

Do you feel like you are constantly walking into a brick wall when it comes to obtaining your dream body? Do you feel like it's out of reach? Do you want to find out how I broke free of this doubt and obtained my dream body?

The majority of people who think about what their dream body is, think about how it looks. When people look in the mirror, it's a constant judging competition, 'ergh these bingo wings, the muffin top, the belly rolls, the non-existent thigh gap,' the list goes on. These feelings suck the life out of your self-worth; they take the focus off what you can actually achieve. I was plagued by these thoughts and don't get me wrong they still creep back in from time to time. However, when I realised that the dream body is more than how much fat I have, it was actually full steam ahead to my aesthetic goals, as well as functional achievements in health and fitness that weren't even planned. I lost over twenty-five pounds; I fell in love with lifting heavy weights and I found the confidence to pose for photos in a sports bra. These are just some of my wins, and I am proud of every single one of them.

Focusing on our actual health is often a secondary reactive thought and not our number one daily priority. It is usually because we are feeling some form of pain, whether it is physical pain in our joints, our lungs as we walk up the stairs or emotional pain in our mental health through stress or anxiety; or through a loved one shocking us with a life-changing diagnosis. It can take years, or a negative health event to escape the dark place, that is the narrow mindedness of focussing on the aesthetic goals of our dream body we want. We don't even realise we are in a dark place. Some people never actually escape that dark place.

But do you know what, it isn't the fault of the individual. It's not like they have sat back and not tried to help themselves get out of the dark place. How I describe the world of health and fitness is like trying to swim from the bottom of the pool for air, while there are constant bricks being thrown at you. You can picture your end goal, but to get there you have to swallow diet pills which make you shit yourself, try thousands of shakes, buy hundreds of fitness influencers $20 workout programs or try the newest diet of only eating apples before midday and pears after midday. Actually, you know what, swap that swimming pool for the deep ocean, with killer sharks, strong currents and throw in a storm too. What I am trying to explain is, the world of health and fitness is as much of a commercialised place as any, how people look and feel is well and truly part of the capitalist world. This means it isn't short of false information, untrustworthy claims and fake news. This in itself has caused negative mental and physical health issues in the general population, but also those who have been sucked into the health and fitness influencer game.

So, you're probably thinking now, 'great Jen, thanks for making my dream body seem unachievable.' Sorry about that, but I want to tell you, there is a way to see through the bullshit. I want to tell you my story of how I went from losing my health both physically and mentally to the corporate world and how I healed myself to achieve my dream body going on to influence hundreds of women to take control of their health too.

Let's go right back and set the scene of my childhood. From a health perspective, my childhood was awesome. I had (and still have) incredible role models, it was filled with lots of nutritious food, I was encouraged to be outside and was given the opportunity to exercise how I wanted to. Whether it was swimming, hockey, gymnastics, hiking… you name it, I most likely tried it during my upbringing.

As a teenager, I was bigger than all my friends, and by bigger, I don't mean fat. I was taller by a good few inches, had a muscly frame and therefore was a few dress sizes bigger. Because I was brought up in a body-positive household, the fact I was bigger didn't bother me one bit. I think it was amazing to have this mindset as a teenager because teenage years are often where eating disorders and body dysmorphic thinking begins, especially these days with the influence of social media. However, this mindset set me up for denial as I became an adult. I moved away from home when I was eighteen, away from the good influences of my family. During this time, I did start to put weight on; I still wasn't necessarily fat and I would say the majority of the weight was literally about growing up into a woman. Yet, this is where my unhealthy behaviours began. This is when I started trying new ways to manage my weight, including different diets and workout plans. I would go and study from 9am and 5pm and live off a couple of breakfast bars, then I would eat a plate of vegetables with some cheddar cheese on; then I would drink a bottle of wine and a few cocktails out with my friends on a night out (most nights of the week). I didn't realise the negative impacts this lifestyle was having on my health.

My true weight gain and decline in health mainly happened when I worked in my corporate job. It was a slow decline over around three years and I didn't realise it was happening. I was fresh out of my Master's degree, excited to start my career in an area I was truly passionate about. I was still dabbling with the gym, still eating vegetables but I wasn't paying attention to over-consuming food in the office and the new sedentary office lifestyle I had entered into (sitting on my [fat] arse all day). I still had that mindset that I wasn't overweight, which I now recognise as complete denial and it was damaging my health. I had low energy, couldn't control my emotions, was in physical pain and had no idea about stress.

It wasn't until I stepped into a new gym, with a supportive

community and a coach who ran fat loss programmes with a no-nonsense approach, that I discovered I had at least twenty-five pounds of unwanted fat and my health was suffering because of it. I was in denial about my digestive issues, eczema flare-ups, mental health problems, aching knees and back and hormonal imbalances. There was also the realisation that this weight gain had knocked my body confidence. I didn't like looking at photos of me dressed up for nights out and I was picky with the type of clothes I would wear. I would untag photos of me, where I could see the lumps and bumps. In these photos, I was happy in the moment, but looking back at my appearance would taint the fond memories I had made with my friends. I had low body confidence and it was pretty tough going sometimes.

This was my turning point. This was when I decided to educate myself; not only on how to lose weight effectively and keep it off but more importantly on other areas of health which were impacting my life. From then on, I made changes and chose to stick to them. I found a way of eating and moving which helped me shift those unwanted pounds and keep them off. I still ate the foods I enjoyed but also realised what my body truly craved was nutritious food, which helped me with my performance goals in the gym and also made me feel happy mentally. Once I had shifted those unwanted pounds, it provided me with two things: the first, it opened my eyes to fixing other areas of my health. The second is what feels like endless opportunities in my life.

To the first point, opening my eyes to fixing other areas of my health. This is an endless journey, but not like the drastic shark-infested ocean I described earlier, but more island hopping on a yacht and the yacht gets more luxurious as you reach each island. This is when I started focussing more on my health and less on the way I looked. I learned lots about mobility by reaching out to sports therapists, physiotherapists and movement specialists; I fixed aches and pains caused by being sat at a desk all day. I learned about my hormones by tracking symptoms and seeking help from hormonal experts. This is the time I discovered mental health is so important. This is the time when I realised that the winter months gave me a massive kick in the teeth every year due to my seasonal affective disorder. But instead of hiding away from it and just accepting that I would feel down every year for four months, I learned how to face it head-on, to prevent the majority of my symptoms but also how to be kind to myself on days when I am low.

Another turning point for my mental health was my ability to manage stress. Modern-day life breeds stress; whether it is with your job, your home life or the news and media. Our bodies and minds are not capable of coping with this amount of unmanaged stress. The ability for me to manage my own stress unlocked freedom for me. Stress is literally the reason I am now a health and fitness coach. The acknowledgement that my full-time corporate job was causing me unnecessary stress, drove me to seek out an alternative lifestyle. It drove me to really dig deep, realising there is more to life than being a number and that you should put yourself first. I realised I was in a job that as much as I tried, I wasn't making a difference. My job was in health, safety and environment therefore you would naturally expect me to feel some sense of achievement through keeping people safe and healthy, and the environment protected. However, the corporate world is all about numbers, and the constant focus on the pound signs dragged me down. I wanted to make a difference, and there was no way of achieving that with the chains that were strapped to my wrists.

Breaking free of those chains, enabled me to reach one of the biggest islands on my health journey and truly level up my yacht. This is when I made my biggest investment in my health, by investing in a business coach. Yes, that's right, a business coach helped me with my mental health. No, they didn't coach me directly in mental health, but that investment provided me with the opportunity to remove the biggest stressor in my life. Taking that huge step to leave my corporate career behind, was one of the best things I have ever done to improve my health.

I want to go into the reasons why it is important for me to share my story and to help steer you to the centre of the health and fitness maze once and for all. I want to reach as many people as possible with the goal of shaping their future to a healthier and happier version. People, especially women, are terrible at putting their health first; and this means they aren't reaching their true potential, therefore neither can their families and those they care for. Ask yourself this question; are you focussing 100% on your health as a number one priority? Do you put your oxygen mask on before you help others put theirs on first? Women are huge role models to people in their lives, which means when they have their health in check, the rest of their world has their health in check too.

According to the World Health Organisation, in 2019, 1.9 billion adults and 390 million children (under 19 years) worldwide were obese, and this number just keeps growing every year. There are more deaths worldwide linked to being overweight and obese than linked to being underweight. However, when was the last time you saw an advert for an overweight kid stating they are malnourished and truly damaging their health versus seeing an advert of an underweight kid who is also malnourished? Deaths associated with obesity and being overweight are ALL PREVENTABLE, literally, every… single… one.

Together we can stop the downward spiral of generations becoming more and more unhealthy through creating as many healthy role models as possible. You just have to look at the obesity crisis which has taken over the world to realise that something needs to be done. People are either ignoring the fact that they are eating or drinking themselves into an early grave or they realise the issue but the right decision of taking control of their health is being drowned out by quick-fix diets, pills, shakes and everyday stressors which can make you more unhealthy, waste your time and your money (yeah, it always comes back to money). I want the world to wake up to the fact that being healthy is easier than not being healthy and that it opens up opportunities that they didn't realise existed.

It is now time to stop swimming through the shark-infested ocean and start island hopping through life. If you are still at stage one, please don't worry, I am now going to share how to get started on your journey to dry land and onwards onto your island-hopping life.

The hard start: what you need to do is draw the line in the sand on the first desert island you land on and make that decision you are going to join the yacht life forever. This isn't easy, this is when you need to give yourself a slap and stop denying yourself of the opportunities that are facing you. You need to write down what your goals are, why you haven't reached them yet, what you have previously tried and why that didn't work, and really admit to yourself what you need to do to get going with your health goals. If the answer to the last question is 'I don't know,' then the actual answer is 'ask for help!'

Ask for help: this step shouldn't be skipped whether you have a solid plan in place or you're still treading water. But you need to choose someone (or more than one person) who is going to help you with getting to your goals. They could be helping you with actually putting the plan in place, advising you on what the next best steps are for your health goals, providing accountability and support throughout your journey to reach a specific goal. Or most importantly being an absolute cheerleader for you. But one thing you need to bear in mind is that you must trust 100% that this person really wants to help you. This person must not be one of those sharks, that'll drag you back into the ocean.

Set SMART goals: set short, medium- and long-term goals. Work backwards; so first, set your long-term goal, this can be twelve months or longer away. Then your medium-term goal: set this at no more than two months, ideally a month. Then ask yourself...what do you need to achieve every month to reach your medium-term goal? This is where your short-term goals come in: what weekly steps do you need to take? These should be easily achievable, for example: drink six glasses of water a day, go for a ten-minute walk at lunchtime, eat five different fruits or 'veggies' every day, etcetera. If you're not sure about goal setting, then refer back to point two.

Be honest, and just to do it: every time you start to make excuses up for not working out, not cooking that healthy meal, not reducing your screen time, etcetera - stop yourself. Ask yourself, 'are my excuses valid?' Don't get me wrong, there will be *some* completely valid excuses. However, let's be really honest, we do have time - sorry (not sorry) - just had to add that one in there. I have clients who literally work 6am to 9pm with three kids and they find time to smash their goals. If you really want it, you'll get there. Say no to excuses.

Reflect and celebrate: this is probably my favourite tip but the most overlooked. This time allows you to reassess your goals, what needs tweaking, what have been your wins then shout them from the rooftops! Literally! Well if you don't want to do that, that's fine, but tell someone, put it on your social media, write it down in a book of wins. I mean *all* wins, even the things that you might see as too small to celebrate: they aren't, be proud of yourself.

Growth: constantly strive for better. I don't mean you have to lose the weight, then become an athlete. But if you want to, kudos. I mean to explore your health further, take a step back and look at my journey; health is physical, mental, emotional and social. It's a huge remit to explore and learn from but, most importantly, to feel better every time you reach a new island.

There are endless opportunities out there when it comes to improving your health. I love working with women who have chosen to finally take control of their health and make the commitment to themselves and their loved ones to get on their first luxurious yacht. I love being a passenger on their journey. I like to make my advice available and provide value to a wide network of women, and this is why I created my favourite place to be on the internet... Female Bosses - Health & Fitness. This is my free Facebook group, where inspiring women from all over the world come to share their stories, ask for support and sail on their yachts as a regatta. I would love it if you also wanted to hop on board the community ship and sail together on our health journeys. You can find us at www.facebook.com/groups/femalebosseshealth. Alternatively, if you want my direct support, I'd love for you to get in touch with me for a free consultation.

About the Author

Jen Harrap is a Health and Fitness Coach with a passion of getting everyone living a healthy lifestyle on their terms. She spent eight years researching the most efficient methods for fat loss, strength gain and mastered it for herself. She then went on to help hundreds of women achieve their own personal health and fitness goals. She is a qualified personal trainer and obesity and diabetes specialist. Jen helps women lose fat and gain strength so they never have to worry about the number on the scales again.

Website: www.jenharrap.com
Facebook:
www.facebook.com/jenharraphealth
www.facebook.com/groups/femalebosseshealth
Email: jen@jenharrap.com.

How a Teacher Paid off 100k in Debt and Gained the Confidence to Live the Life of Her Dreams

By Mary-Ellen Fimbel

Hello! First, I wanted to say I am so excited that you are reading this book! The other authors and I want to empower you to make the changes to give you the life you desire no matter your current circumstance. We are sharing our stories to inspire you to open your mind to the truth that you can have the life you want. We hope through this book you feel empowered to create your own life story that supports the true, amazing, and successful you.

My story is about money, making it, and then using it to make meaningful moves that have improved my quality of life. I hope that in these next few pages you find some inspiration to get your money moving meaningfully. If you are looking for more help or inspiration, I hope you will join my Facebook group Fundamental Finance: Community Committed to Change.

I graduated college in May 2010, it was a hot and beautiful day. Most of my friends were so excited to be graduating and heading off into the "real world". I however was very sad and nostalgic. College had been the one time in my life where I hadn't had much to worry about. Sure, I had struggled and grown personally in college, but it was a break from the responsibility I had faced growing up. My mom suffered from chronic illness, leaving much responsibility to me for taking care of myself and my siblings. Due to high medical costs in the United States, my parents were burdened with significant debt from her health issues and a few other unwise money moves. This caused much stress in our home and I was often put in the middle of my parents' disagreements and had contributed several times to bills to avoid further issues. I often served as the phone screener to collectors, who were not easily convinced I was a kid. College had been a welcome break from all that. A time to really focus on learning and figuring out who I wanted to become, how I could make good decisions, and escape stressful living.

It was no surprise that I was stressed about what life had in store for me after graduation. Specifically, what worried me was that I had turned down my first job offer. As I sat there in the sun, side by side with the other music majors I had spent the better part of four years with, I wondered if I had made the right choice. I wondered if I would get another job offer or If I would have to move back in with my parents until the debt collectors for my student loans came and threw me in jail, or worse. I wasn't really sure what worse was, but I knew I might end up there if I couldn't pay my debts.

The offer I had received was teaching at a low-income school in a little town five hours away from home. I had grown up just outside a small town but still pretty near a big city. The district that extended the offer was deep in the middle of nowhere. Still, I wasn't as worried about the location as I was about the salary.

Adding to my stress, the car that my friend had graciously sold me when she left to teach abroad (for much less than it was worth) had finally kicked the bucket. I would need reliable transportation to accept any job. Unlike most of my peers, my college expenses and transportation were funded by me, not my parents. People who knew my situation made me doubt my decision to turn down the job. Should I have taken the offer and tried to make it work, tried to find a way to fix that old car, or just live where I could walk to work? Would that even be possible in such a remote location? The math just didn't work. With the minimum payment on my loans, and a car, I wouldn't have enough left to eat. And yet, "Take the job, you just graduated and need the experience", was the advice I had heard from most of my family and friends. They said I would figure things out after I started working. No one seemed to take the loans as seriously as I did.

I also had just started dating my boyfriend and many people were concerned that I had turned down the job because of him. This was not a concern for me, I was too responsible to let my heart influence my decision. I had gone for an interview and I loved the school and the position, the staff seemed great, and the town wasn't all that bad. In fact, I could see myself growing an awesome elementary music program there.

Still trying to convince myself I wasn't an idiot for turning down a job, I walked the stage, graduated, and began life in the "real world".

The first two months of that summer, I was filled with worry and anxiety about how I was going to manage if I didn't get a job. I realized I had to pay attention not just to the job opportunities, but also to the salaries. This wasn't too hard since teacher salaries are public information, but I was surprised to learn how widely the starting salaries varied from district to district. Initially, I had looked at smaller districts because I thought that was the type of community I wanted to live in. However, I quickly discovered I would have to focus on larger districts that paid higher rates for first-year teachers. Hundreds of applications and a half dozen interviews later I emerged with what I felt like was an acceptable job offer: $40,000 a year with a signing bonus I could use as my emergency fund. A side benefit: it was only forty-five minutes from home and two hours from my boyfriend.

That first year of teaching was hard. Even though the job paid more than the first offer, I struggled with making progress on my student loans. In addition to the student loans, I had been forced to purchase a new car. I found that car dealers cannot finance used cars as easily as new ones. I had neither enough cash to buy a drivable used car or fix the car my friend had sold me. Buying a brand-new car enabled me to accept the job offer I had received. I needed something reliable to get to work and manage the teaching position I had accepted, which was split between two campuses each day. But the payments still added to the weight of my debt burden. I decided to enjoy the new car and find a way to pay it off quickly.

Fortunately, by the end of the year, I was feeling more confident in both managing my money and teaching. I had been able to keep up with a budget and saved enough to allow me to pay all my bills a month ahead. This took away the stress of feeling like I was running out of money at the end of each month. I had taken the signing bonus and created an emergency fund, had cash flowed a few health expenses, and made a bit of progress on my car. I also allowed myself the luxury of keeping my apartment cool during the extreme heat of Texas summer. As a teacher, I had improved in classroom management and lesson planning and had a better grasp of elementary repertoire. I knew I had made the right choice in declining that first offer. I never would have been able to afford a car and the student loan payments on that salary and that position would not have provided as much training in elementary music. With this new confidence, I made some important decisions that began setting myself up for some real financial success.

When I graduated, I had some basic advice in personal finance that helped me get off to a good start. My friend's mom had introduced me to Dave Ramsey in the summer of 2009 and his program seemed promising. It at least gave me the idea that people do get out of debt. I read some critiques of him and his program and got the idea that either I could pay down debt snowball style (smallest to largest, as recommended by Dave) or by interest rate, which other experts favored. The more immediate gratification and simplicity of the snowball was more my style so that's what I started with. I knew the only way to expedite progress was to earn more, which was also suggested by Dave and just about anyone else I read. But as a teacher, I couldn't just go negotiating a raise or working overtime, which were some of the main suggestions for expediting paying down debt. As a music teacher, I also had extra rehearsals and performances that interfered with getting a second job. And It was important for me to keep my weekends free to visit my boyfriend. I knew I had to be a little more creative about making extra money. I signed up for tutoring after school a couple of days a week and I got a position assisting the director of the district's children's choir, both of these small jobs helped make progress on paying off my debt and also kept me busy and away from activities that would have increased my spending.

Live like a college student until you are not paying for college

"If for any reason decide you must take out a loan for college, you should continue to live like a poor college student until it is paid off. This is because the reason poor college students are poor is because they are paying for college." - Unknown

This perspective gave me hope. Most proponents of debt-free college suggest living at home and cutting commuting costs. Neither of these options would have been practical or possible since my parents lived far from any college campus and I did not have a car. I did end up taking out student loans. Around $45,000 worth.

Inspired by that author's advice after graduation I kept my lifestyle similar to when I was in college. The two big differences were that I bought a car and rented an apartment. I felt conflicted about both of these choices. As I mentioned above, I would have rather bought a cheaper used car, but I couldn't get finance for one because of my lack of credit. Somehow I was able to get approved for an additional $16,000 for a new car, in spite of my lack of credit, but not $9,000 for a used car. You figure that one out. I was also paying over $700 a month for a one-bedroom apartment. I had seen cheaper places but this one was closer to both my schools.

I tried hard to keep my other expenses small in the spirit of living like a college student. I didn't spend a lot on furnishing my apartment. I made good use of some milk crates I had acquired. I gratefully accepted some curb-side finds from my uncle and found $50 worth of furniture at a church garage sale. It wasn't much, but it turns out when you live alone and work a lot you don't really need much in the way of furniture. The only thing I really missed was a real bed. I also kept my grocery budget low and only went out to eat once a week for lunch and occasionally when visiting my boyfriend. I kept up this basic lifestyle until I paid off my car two and a half years later.

Don't pay too much to sleep

The number one thing that has helped me make financial progress on a lower income is choosing housing wisely. For me, this meant roommates. This has also been true for my siblings who are also on their way to financial freedom. They saw how choosing roommates to split housing costs helped me win and they followed suit. In my first year of teaching, I made slow progress on paying off debt because of the cost of the rent. In 2010, $700 was about average for my location, but it was easy for me to see it was my biggest expense, and the one I had the power to change. In the summer of 2011, I started thinking about how I was living differently than I was in college and I realized the biggest thing was I didn't have a roommate. I began searching online to find a different living situation but after several inquiries were met with photos more revealing of the potential "roommates" than the actual living spaces, I decided against living with random internet people.

Luckily just as my second year of teaching started a friend got hired in my district and she was excited at the prospect of living together. We lived about a month in my one-bedroom together and then decided to move to a two-bedroom unit that cost about $900 a month. The two bedrooms were vastly different sizes. I negotiated so that my friend could have the larger room and pay a bit more and I could have the smaller room and pay less. Since she was still paying less than she would for a one-bedroom apartment, she was happy with the deal. This allowed me to cut my rent down to $400. Sure, I had a little less space, but it was more than enough. My bedroom in the shared apartment was way smaller than I had had living alone, but really I only slept there since I worked a lot. This was my first experience with assuming a little more risk for a lot more gain. The inconvenience of the small space was worth it for the progress I was making on my loans.

People thought I was crazy. Perhaps I was, but I made progress. By spring break of 2013, I had paid off my $16,000 car! I took a little break from total frugality and splurged on a touch screen music player. Then I got back to action and kept paying down my student loans. Finally, I achieved my next big goal of total debt freedom in 2015, five years after I had begun teaching.

Put your ME in MEaningful

Three years after becoming debt-free I began to get really frustrated with my husband. By 2018 we had cash flowed a wedding, a baby, and adult braces for both my husband and myself, all while killing my husband's $55,000 worth of student loans. But his company had reorganized, leaving him without a job, so he had become a stay at home dad. This was a change from our original plan of having me stay home once we were debt-free. I wanted to be at home with my two-year-old son, but instead, he was the one getting to be a stay at home parent. Additionally, I felt trapped in my job and wanted a change. I was so caught up in being frustrated with my husband that I missed out on how lucky we were to be able to have one parent staying home and how much my son was benefiting from it. I was feeling trapped by our tight budget and lack of progress in investing. Also, I really wanted to do some traveling. I wasn't getting to use any of my income for what I thought I wanted. This meant I was working without meaning.

In February of 2017, we had gotten a much larger tax return than expected: $3,000. We decided it could be put towards a big vacation once my husband was back working, and until then it would be good padding towards our emergency fund. A few months later, my brother accepted his dream job in Germany, and I promised we would visit him. I had thought surely by the summer of 2018 my husband would have a job and things would stabilize so we could go.

Back then I didn't see myself as the provider for our family. Even though my income had always been more than my husband's I had adopted the old-fashioned mindset that the husband should provide. Unfortunately, this prevented me from seeing the power I had in the situation.

At this point, I had tied our ability to travel and enjoy ourselves with my husband's employment, even though I knew we could make it on my income.

By January of 2018, my husband was still unemployed and I was really upset about not getting to travel after working so hard to kill my debt. I decided that even if I went alone, I was going to find a way to visit my brother in Germany! I started investigating flights, and what I discovered was that rather than the $1,500 a person I expected to pay in airfare, I could find tickets for much less. I started watching deals and decided if I could get tickets for all of us for less than $2,000 we could all go.

After about five months of research and a lot of doubt and anxiety,

I booked our first family trip and my first major international adventure. I paid about $1,600 for airfare and $1,300 for a nice hotel, and that summer we spent an amazing two weeks in Munich. The trip for the three of us including airfare and the hotel was about $3,500. I've seen others travel for less, but it was really good for my first international trip and it really helped me feel aligned with my life again. I wanted to travel, and I wanted to spend this kind of time with my family. The success of that trip helped prepare me for learning about world-schooling and helped my husband and I realize how much we value time together. This planted the seeds for moving out of our traditional life and into our extraordinary life.

Financial independence isn't the same as retiring early

While budgeting for our wedding, I had discovered the FIRE (Financial Independence Retire Early) movement. At that time, it was mostly techy white guys who made what I considered a ton of money ($100,000 a year or more), who didn't spend it, invested it, and retired at around the age of thirty by living off the dividends. I learned from the now famous financial blogger Mr. Money Mustache that this could be done on any income with the right balance of lifestyle and investing. With both my husband and I working, our numbers we had been putting towards our debt were pretty close to the amount he recommended to FIRE in ten years or less. So, we had decided that would be our plan after we became debt-free and paid for the wedding. Due to my husband's job situation, or lack thereof, we weren't able to continue putting as much away as we needed to after 2017 and though our trip in 2018 had made me realize we were still saving more and had more opportunities than most, I didn't fully realize the freedom we had given ourselves until the summer of 2020.

In the fall of 2019, my husband received a job offer the same day I gave birth to our daughter. This was a relief as teachers are not given paid maternity leave and it would have been pretty rough for me to take much time off after her birth without him working. It was a very stressful transition to him being back at work since my son had grown accustomed to being home with his dad. Furthermore, the cost of daycare for two was a much larger percentage of my husband's check than we had hoped. By the time I returned to work, we were already discussing if both of us working was really the best option for our family.

In March of 2020 COVID came and schools went virtual. My district was one of the few I felt like was doing a phenomenal job of keeping kids and teachers safe and allowing teachers to do their best with virtual learning and teaching from home.

By April, we had evaluated daycare costs and decided my husband would resign at the end of the summer as the financial benefits to him working were not worth the mental and emotional strain on our family. However, in early July it turned out schools would return to in-person learning. I got scared. I had a health condition that made me high risk for complications from COVID and as an elementary music teacher, I would see every kid in the school regularly. Between the actual risk of the virus and the risk of accidentally transmitting it to my family or any number of students, I knew I couldn't go back to in-person right away and considered resigning. But then our district decided to start the year virtually, so I stayed.

By late July, more changes had been made and it looked as though teachers would have to return to school to teach, even if they were teaching virtually unless they applied for special permissions. I doubted whether I should apply since I wasn't sure how that would even work for a music teacher. Additionally, I had already started hearing that most applications to remain virtual from home were being denied so I almost didn't turn one in. But at the last minute, I decided to. I knew if I was denied I could still resign so I might as well try.

It was then that I realized because of our financial choices, having no debt and a well-funded emergency fund, we were in a position to make choices. I wasn't trapped in a job, I had choices. We had savings to last us long enough for me to find another path. It sounded crazy to say that in the middle of a pandemic, but it was true.

With that confidence, we also had my husband resign without knowing how long I would be able to work from home. Our kids could be home with him and safe from daycare, and we took control of our lives. We were free to choose to put our health and safety ahead of our jobs which is something I knew many people were not able to do.

By November, stress on teachers was unreal, and I knew I was dealing with less than many teachers. That's when I knew I had to share my story of how I found freedom through smart financial planning. I want everyone to be able to put the health, physical and mental, and safety of their families before their jobs. That's why I started FUNdamental Finance to help people learn that getting control of their money isn't just possible, it's also seriously fun. You can check out my Facebook group to learn some great ways to start getting your money on the right track.

Freedom in life through focused finances

By stepping up to the role of provider and taking control of my money, I set up a lifestyle that allows us to roll with the punches and gives us choices in tough times. When my husband was out of work for two years our lifestyle suffered very little. We even ended up being able to take an awesome trip. When I realized how much I needed to take that trip to Germany things lined up easily and the trip was fun and relaxing because we had a budget and stuck to it. When the pandemic came and I didn't feel comfortable having the kids in daycare, we were able to keep them home. I was also confident enough to ask for a virtual teaching position, knowing that I could still quit if they denied me. Now I'm continuing to align my life and money with my own amazing financial coaching business which allows me to help other people align their lifestyles to optimize freedom and happiness.

If you would like help getting into the winning mindset and a place to learn the skills you need to succeed with your money, come and join the Facebook group – Fundamental Finance: Community Committed to Change for some free training and a great support community. We would love to have you!

About the Author

Mary-Ellen Fimbel is a teacher-of-all-trades who loves engaging with students in the classroom, the great outdoors, and online. She believes that learning should be accessible to everyone and that people learn best when engaging with their own interests. She brings that philosophy to a wide range of subjects, from musical concepts to 3-D printing, and now financial coaching.

Mary-Ellen and her husband have paid off all of their debt including student loans (yes, all of them), totaling more than $100,000. They've also cash-flowed their way through $42,000 of wedding and medical expenses, proving that living debt-free on a teacher's income is absolutely possible.

Mary-Ellen knows that personal finance is a confusing and sometimes scary world, but she's passionate about coaching people towards the freedom and security that comes with financial stability.

Facebook: www.facebook.com/groups/4893484904026208
Email: brainsbeforebudgets@gmail.com

Passion Alone Isn't Enough To Build A Successful Business

By Aileen Lane

"You'll never make money as a personal stylist!"

I heard this comment more than once over the years.

My family seemed especially determined to let me know!

I dreaded when it came around to that time at family get-togethers when I was asked how my business was doing. I'd try to have my answer ready or even tell them to mind their own business but it was still a source of great shame that I couldn't make much more than pocket money as a personal stylist. They all thought I was a bit mad.

I wasn't always a personal stylist you see; I had a stable career and a great salary before I decided to take a big leap of faith and follow my dreams.

Let me take you right back to the start...

One of eleven kids and the oldest girl, with eight younger siblings, I seemed to be put in charge of everyone from an early age. It makes me laugh now because I was totally unaware that I was known as a bit of a bossy boots when I was growing up.

I was often required to babysit, get my brothers and sisters organised for school and help them with their homework.

When I was in school, I didn't wait to be invited to any of the other girls' gangs; fancy paper and hopscotch were all the rage at the time. Instead, I set up my own team and went about organising activities that me and my bunch wanted to participate in; rounders or some other running activity were more my thing.

In my final year in secondary school, I was awarded 'student of the year'. This is an award for the most popular final year student as voted by the students and teachers. It was quite the honour and I can appreciate it now, but at the time, the whole thing embarrassed me. I wasn't quite ready to take the lead yet!

From an early age, I was impatient and could always see opportunities and more innovative ways of doing things. I often ran before I could walk. Nothing motivated me more than having a goal and reaching that goal. Coming up with new ideas and taking the lead seemed to come naturally to me, though this didn't always enamour me to my various managers and coaches along the way. When I look back now, I realise that I wasn't always the easiest employee. Some people were born to run their own show and I fall clearly into that category, though it took me a few goes to find my feet and my voice.

When I left school, I pursued a Degree in Biotechnology and then went on to do a Master's in Food Engineering. While the industry didn't exactly excite me, it seemed practical at the time as there were lots of life science companies in Ireland. I did get a job when I finished my Master's and my first 'real job' was in a small start-up pasta company in Naas, County Kildare. I was hired as a supervisor down on the manufacturing floor. It was a bit of a baptism by fire as I had zero practical experience, so I learnt a lot on the job in the year I spent there. Telling people what to do seemed to come naturally to me, though it didn't always make me popular.

Originally from Ireland, I have spent much of my adult life as an expat. After leaving my first 'proper job', I joined my then-boyfriend (my husband now for 17 years) and I spent my first year away from home working as a manufacturing manager in a dairy plant in Bahrain in the Middle East. I was the only woman in manufacturing, everything was new and different but I braved my fears and came out the other end a lot more savvy. I even learnt how to drive, though my dad would argue with this, and I got my license during the time I spent on the desert island.

In January 2000, we moved to Singapore as my husband got a job with one of the big accounting firms there. It was a massive change from Bahrain and we both loved the cleanliness, excitement and opportunities afforded to us by the little red dot. I got a job as a process manager in an infant formula plant within weeks of arriving, so we settled quickly and it became home almost immediately. I spent six years working in manufacturing and product development. I had amazing opportunities to visit different countries and meet lots of people from different cultures and backgrounds. I learnt how to problem solve and how to be professional in my years at Wyeth.

One day, the HR people in Wyeth invited the Image Consultant Jill Lowe of Colour Me Beautiful, to come and do a talk about making the most of your physical appearance by wearing the right colours. I sat there in the audience mesmerised by the impact of colour. The seeds were planted and I seemed to see colour everywhere after that. I got my colours done with my mum soon after that and I was hooked. I quietly studied as a colour and style consultant during my evenings and weekends and declared I was starting my own business soon after getting my qualifications. Oh, the innocence! I thought my passion for colour and style was all I needed but I was soon to learn that it required a little more than that.

I left my high paying manufacturing job on the last day of February 2006 and opened the doors to my new company Nutri-Style on 1st March 2006.

I took out an expensive office on Orchard Road, possibly the most expensive place you could choose to have your office in Singapore and sat there looking at the phone that never rang for months. I blew through my savings within six months and even had to get a loan from my family to keep going. I can still feel the shame of failure. I will be ever thankful to my husband, parents and brother who bailed me out in those early days and kept a roof over my head. It was at this point that I knew I had to get real and start making money. It was extraordinarily difficult though, as I had pretty much no business skills. While many image consulting training courses provide fantastic technical skills in colour and style, there was little or no training or support around getting clients.

It took me years of trial and error, and long hours to figure out how to, first, make enough to cover the rent and slowly start to turn a profit. I tried adding all sorts of income streams, and I realise now that this was part of my problem. I provided everything from weight loss services to 'The Polished Professional' workshops for large corporations. I was a 'Jack of all trades' but master of none; I was exhausted from trying to serve everyone! No one knew exactly what I was providing, least of all myself. As time went on, I started to make a name for myself as a talented colour consultant and several personal stylists approached me to teach them my method as they were confused by the colour training they received. I began to train consultants in seasonal colour analysis in 2010. I had niched down without really even being aware of the concept.

Despite loving what I was doing and after 8 years in the business, I was still not making as much money as I had made in my corporate job, despite working long hours. However, I loved my job and the transformation I saw in my clients' confidence kept me going. I also had invested so much that it was hard to just give up at this point. The Universe has a way of nudging us along though, and change was about to happen quicker than I expected.

I had my first son in 2009 and my second in 2012. My second son wasn't a good sleeper and I ended up having to put my business on hold for a few years, as it just wasn't possible to run a business with my family demands at the time. I ended up working part time in my husband's business for over 4 years and I learnt some valuable business skills during that time.

My life was turned upside down in March 2017, when I lost my beloved younger brother to suicide. With just a year and three months between us, we grew up side-by-side. We started school, smoked our first cigarette and attended our first disco together. We even had our first children within three weeks of each other. It's hard to explain grief until you experience it but it became immediately crystal clear what was important to me. My husband and I decided to move closer to Ireland, so we could visit our families more often and spend more time at home.

After eighteen years of living and working in Singapore, my family and our dog Hazelnut moved to a beautiful village in the South of France in December 2017.

Initially, I tried to get a job in manufacturing but, with only schoolgirl French and being out of the food industry for many years, I didn't have much luck. I also considered going back to image consulting but while I loved the industry, I was reluctant to start all over again knowing how difficult it is to make a decent income as a personal stylist.

Despite this, the urge to get back into the industry wouldn't go away, so I decided to give image consulting another go and set up my company Lane Image Consulting in September 2018. This time I was determined to make it financially viable, so I approached it as a business rather than a hobby. I studied different business models and was much more business savvy this time around.

I quickly realised that using the old business model of promoting myself through talks and events wasn't going to work in a small village, where the majority of people only speak French. It forced me to consider going online (way before Covid). Once I opened my mind to the possibilities, I realised that I had all the skills I needed right there in front of me - don't we always! Online colour analysis was the way forward for me. It made so much sense. It was the 'a-ha' moment Oprah talks about.

After lots of research and establishing an online process to conduct online colour analysis, I set about putting a plan together to get my first clients. I quickly realised that working from pictures was just not enough. It was missing the human connection and communication. The client missed the experience of talking about their colours and to be honest, I was bored to death looking at pictures and not connecting with people.

The doubts started to creep in. Does online colour analysis really work? I was also worried that I would excommunicate myself from the image consulting community, as online colour analysis was a new frontier at the time and there was a lot of negativity and naysayers around the topic. I even had other personal stylists come on my social media posts and put harmful comments. I couldn't quite believe that people would actually do that. That's social media for you - once you start putting yourself out there, you have to expect that not everyone will love you. True to form though, the more resistance I saw, the more I could see the opportunity, so I persisted.

I decided to introduce a one-hour online consultation with the client to discuss my findings in their personalised report and there was an immediate turnaround.

I loved it and more importantly, the client loved it.

The testimonials started to roll in and I knew I was onto an absolute winner.

It felt so good to finally be doing what I loved every day and also to have a steady flow of clients.

All of a sudden my client base became the world, rather than the English speaking community in a small village in the South of France. I could also get back in touch with all my Singapore connections and let them know that I was available for business.

I was so excited and my adrenaline was through the roof. I could 'do colours' every day to my heart's content, from anywhere in the world, with all the flexibility I wanted.

Getting more clients and having a consistent and reliable income was great but the real joy was in realising that I could help other personal stylists avoid all the pitfalls I had encountered, by showing them how to take their colour business online and shortcut their journey to success! My 5 Weeks To Online Colour Expert program has been turning out online colour consultants for over two years now and it's still my most popular online course. You can get started in Online Colour Analysis here with my Free Online Colour Analysis Training.

I also train personal stylists to conduct style consultations online without having to take measurements or having to pay for expensive licenced style guides. You can watch this free webinar here to learn how you can take your styling services online.

My mission for the past few years has been to assist talented personal stylists to become savvy business women because that's what they need to be to have consistent 5K, 10K or 20K months. You will often hear me saying, "you need to be a savvy business woman first and a personal stylist second'. Unfortunately, this is poorly understood when we start our journey in the image industry. The majority of personal stylists have our own business and need to get our own clients. There is no knight on a white horse standing by to rescue us; we need to do it ourselves.

There are many consultants still selling one-off colour and style services to their clients, which I believe is not a sustainable business model long-term and allows no room for scaling. These consultants are run ragged trying to get clients in the door and spend long hours working for little financial return. I developed my Savvy Stylists Business Academy to take personal stylists from selling one-off lower value services to becoming experts in their niche and creating a high value online program, with a lead generation system that allows them to have a steady flow of high-paying clients and consistent income.

There is no question in my mind that the future of personal stylists is online. The arrival of the Covid pandemic sped up this process but now that many consultants have made the transition, they can see the possibilities and advantages of working online. From being able to work from any location in the world to having access to millions of people who want and need their services.

The online world allows personal stylists to be ultra-niche and work in their zone of genius so they are not competing with other consultants flogging the same old services of colour, style and wardrobe audits. The face of the image consulting industry has changed forever and it's never going back. This terrain is new for lots of consultants though, and they will need to learn new skills to make a success of their online business. The good news is that I witness personal stylists get online, get high paying clients and have a reliable and steady income every day. It's totally possible to make a fantastic living from being a personal stylist but you do need to learn the skills of the online world and how it operates.

As I wrap up my story, there is no question that my background in manufacturing and as an expat has influenced how I choose to live, work and teach. My teaching philosophy is to keep it simple, lead by example and to provide step-by-step guidance to my clients so that they reach your goals by taking the path of least resistance. All my programs prepare you to be able to operate from any location because I know how rewarding and fun it is to travel and work from anywhere in the world. Right now, as I type these words, I am in Ireland visiting my parents. I spend my summers in Ireland as I like to have my two boys (who were born in Singapore) experience Irish culture. Having the freedom to work remotely allows me to have everything I want to experience yet still have a consistent and lucrative income. It brings me great joy to be able to mentor personal stylists from every corner of the globe to do the same. I know now that every experience I had, bad and good, needed to happen to get me to where I am today. I look forward to the next part of my journey as I reach back and help other personal stylists get online, get more clients and make a financial success of their business so they can have everything they deserve and want in their lives as they transform the lives of others for the better.

About the Author

Aileen Lane is a Business Coach to personal stylists. Originally from Ireland, she lived in Singapore for eighteen years before settling in her current location in the South of France. She has spent the last fifteen plus years honing her skills as a trainer and coach within the image industry. She is a certified colour and style consultant and holds Certified Image Professional status with The Association of Image Consultants International. She mentors talented personal stylists to find their zone of genius and to design, create and sell a unique online program so that they can have consistent and lucrative income working from anywhere in the world.

Website: www.laneimageconsulting.com
Facebook:
www.facebook.com/groups/SavvyPersonalStylistsNetwork
Email: aileen@laneimageconsulting.com

Prioritizing Your Presence Without the BS: Mindgoals for Entrepreneurs

By Kelsy Anderson Hoerauf, LMFT

First of all, let me state clearly that the mental health stigma in society is bullshit. I don't even know if the editor will let me keep that word in there, but it is. It's BS for so many reasons, not the least being the fact that it discourages or prevents people who need treatment from getting it. Either they don't try, due to the stigma or even when they do get treatment, they're judged harshly by friends and family. If this is you then I'd like to say hey, you are not alone. I get it! You are strong for reaching out for help, not weak, especially if you are a new mama and suffer from postpartum depression or overwhelm. Mental health symptoms must be viewed as the same as physical health symptoms. Have you ever heard someone telling a person with a broken arm that it's not "real?" I didn't think so. I encourage you to do your part in chipping away at the stigma. I am not my diagnosis and neither are you. We all face trials, some of ours just happen to be of the mental health variety. Read on for more.

I want to explore a personal mental crisis and the system for helping new moms that came out of it. This was different from anything I'd experienced before. It occurred in adulthood and took years to "resolve". Take a deep breath. I'd like to talk about postpartum depression (PPD). For me, it crept up on me slowly over time. I didn't connect the violent thoughts of my death after giving birth to be related to postpartum. And I expressed my concerns to a psychiatrist who did nothing, telling me that because I was already on an antidepressant that I should be fine when it came to postpartum symptoms. This simply turned out to be untrue. Yes, a lie. I felt lied to. Just to be clear, starting within six months of giving birth, (a traumatic birth story, I'll save that for another day) I began having thoughts of suicide, like images and envisioning it. These really disturbing thoughts continued. I kept ignoring and brushing them off thinking they'd disappear soon. Because I took no action toward hurting myself, it seemed easy for medical professionals to dismiss my angst about the thoughts. But the thoughts did not get better, they only got worse. I was distressed for over two years before finally being so overwhelmed by the violent, intrusive thoughts that I checked myself into the psychiatric hospital. If you are suffering with any type of depression signs after having a child, I'm with you! Keep asking for help until someone LISTENS. You deserve to be heard and heeded. In that vein, I'll do my part to encourage health.

As a result of what happened to me, I am very sensitive to new moms and their mental health. As a coach, I don't treat PPD clinically any longer, but I do serve moms as a coach who won't hesitate to recommend treatment if any issues arise. Did I mention that it took me over 2 years to get help? That should not happen. Again, we run into the stigma, which extends not only to the mental health of the mother but also to how she's doing overall. We're told to "enjoy every moment" of our maternity leave. As if we're not SO exhausted and completely run down by caring for our baby. It's a draining time that has its wonderful moments but also has its overly tired ones. If you are there, have been there or will soon be a new mama, take care of yourself and if you want to change careers after having your little one, please come talk to me.

Besides having the intrusive thoughts, I was doing pretty well after maternity leave. I went back to work full time at a clinic that was about a forty-five-minute drive from where we lived. Then I did the math...you know what I'm referring to - the mama math. I'd be gone from home for nine to ten hours per day, five days per week. The question, "can I stay home?" was at the forefront of my mind. It's HARD, don't let anyone tell you this should be easy. Or at least it was hard until I made up my mind.

Let me paint you a picture: me, in my boss' office after giving her a doctor's note stating I should work six hours, two days per week due to mental health reasons (remember that PPD?) She stares at her computer stating, "if you only work six hours you don't get (a break or) a lunch, I don't know if you knew that." I became livid! How was I expected to see back to back clients without any kind of break or lunch?!!? Do you want to see a therapist that's been seeing patients back-to-back for five hours? I knew I couldn't, at least not well, and I pride myself on doing things as excellently as possible. The interaction showed me that I didn't matter to this company. I was just a number. So, I left. Packed up everything that was mine (wall art, office chair) and left. (I'm sure I looked crazy to anyone in the lobby, rolling by with kids' games and large framed art.) The moral of the story is that I quit my job. I recognize I was lucky to be able to do this because of my family situation (dual income), but even if I hadn't been, I was determined to find a way out.

From here I developed the system called M.I.N.D.G.O.A.L.S. combining mindfulness (a process I've used with TONS of clients) and goal setting with a sensitivity to what's going on mentally and emotionally for the mamas I work with. Each letter stands for one step or aspect of healing and moving forward toward being her best self. For a pretty document version of these steps go to http://bit.ly/KelsyFreebie.

M stands for mindful mindset; I for Identify possibilities and the role of self; N stands for Number ideas and select the top one or two to work on (simplify); D for dump old thinking; G for goal definition, personal and business; Ohm meditate daily; A for action steps; L for Lay out steps, schedule and track; S for spirituality, which is a part of any change and everything. Now that I've given you the short and quick version, let's explore each aspect more deeply. You can work on this on your own or with me as your coach. I love guiding women through this process. When you're really engaged in it, incredible growth and shifts occur.

Mindful mindset is very powerful and has two ideas tied to it. First, mindfulness, which is present moment awareness, is vital. The more mindful you are the more mental health benefits you reap. These include less depression, decreased anxiety, and feeling more balanced without being tied to a specific outcome. (Do I sound like a therapist? Haha! Thankfully I can engage in mindfulness coaching and not be "doing therapy".) Regarding mindfulness, the more you can be okay within yourself, the better you can concentrate on the task at hand. To get started with mindfulness you can download a meditation app such as Insight Timer, Headspace, or any of the dozen other meditation apps, to try different types of meditation and different guide voices until you find what fits for you.

The second part, mindset, is something life coaches talk about all the time, but I take it from a psychological standpoint due to my therapist background. Mindset not only refers to what you think but also how you talk to yourself (in your mind) and the way you approach challenges. If you have a positive, go-get-it mindset you are more likely to achieve it than someone with a negative or self-defeating mindset. I realize this is simple but I think it bears repeating, your mindset needs to be mindful, positive and self-affirming if you are going to reach your goals. Just start by noticing the things you are saying to yourself. Are you talking to yourself how you'd talk to a friend? Or are you mean, harsh and derogatory? DO NOT move on to the next step until you start the process of getting a better, more clear and positive mindset. I suggest meditations, affirmations and transformational journaling to help you get mentally fit to own your own business and be a leader, both at home and "at work" even as you work from home.

I stands for identify possibilities and the role of self. Again, this step has two parts. Once your mindset has improved, it is time to list ALL the possibilities available to you for your life and that of your little ones. I mean *all*. No holds barred. For me, I want to live the life of a snowbird, spending a significant part of the winter on a warm, sunny beach. This is a possibility I see for myself. Don't stop short. I could add having a second home on an island or near the beach, driving a Mercedes, etcetera. Nothing is off-limits and if you hear your voice of limiting beliefs crop up, tell it to be quiet! The second part "Identify the role of self" is where you answer the question, "why hasn't this happened yet?" If you are mindfully working toward your goal and you have limiting beliefs come up, for example, "I can't afford beach vacations because I don't work at an agency doing therapy," then go ahead and work through those. Journal it out or touch base with me or your coach. The role of self is so vital I could write a book about just that, but I won't. Suffice it to say, I cannot overemphasize the role of self. I always heard it said that you must become the successful person first, then the success (money, lifestyle) will follow. I encourage you to try it out. You know being you now doesn't work, so become her and see what happens!

N stands for number goal areas and select the top one or two to work toward. Listen up. This is important, you can only pick one or two! This is so challenging as a new entrepreneur. I remember when I thought I needed a business Facebook page, a Facebook group, A YouTube channel, an Instagram strategy, and Twitter as I was just starting out. Do you see how that would feel overwhelming and daunting? I know it feels like everything is so important but it all can't be. You need to narrow it down to mindfully make progress in one area before jumping to the next. If you are doing the daily activities to move your business forward then it will progress even if some lesser tasks aren't prioritized. If you are in the moment, doing what is needed, then you can progress without too much stress. It's when we aren't mindful and say to ourselves that we must do EVERYTHING that we end up overwhelmed and feeling trapped. It is a lot, but you can navigate things. You are not trapped. You can do this. When in doubt, go back to focusing on who you are becoming.

D is for Dump old thinking. Let me tell you about my *old thinking* that I let stick around and stink everything up! It has to do with my worth. I knew what to charge as a therapist and was unsure how this converted or didn't convert to my new role as a life coach. I kept doubting or charging too little because I was "new" at this. But I wasn't new to working with people and helping. I'd been doing it professionally for over ten years. Yet the self-doubt continued until I accepted that I have to charge what I'm worth and not every person is a good client. I had to put myself back in the driver's seat! It relates to mindfulness of who you're becoming and how she thinks. You can't take your negative thought pattern into your new, successful life. There's no room for her, the negative Nancy (sorry if your name is Nancy). Another illustration from my life is that I used to think that I couldn't do certain things because of my mental illness. Now, it is true that I have some limitations because of it, but I have so many more options and possibilities, like being a coach and an author. This again ties into the role of self. Are you building your inner voice to be a cheerleader or a critic? You can have either and it is possible to choose, with some work. This work is vital and if you get nothing else out of this chapter, please know that you can and should dump your old thinking, replacing it with positivity or more neutral thoughts.

G is for goal definition. This pertains to both personal and business goals. I strongly recommend that you have one of each. I have getting movement once to twice per day, (yoga, karate, run/dance) every day as a goal, along with going live every other day including once per week on my personal page plus up to daily in my Kelsy's Bad@$$ Coaching and Counseling group. The personal goal should support the professional goal. Who you are becoming is so much more than hitting a certain goal weight or sales goal, though it's nice to note these along the way. Being mindfully in the moment and focusing on just one personal and one business goal is aimed to help you simplify. If I tried to do it all at once, I'd fail too! Let me illustrate the way a goal has to align with who you are. Another illustration is that I've tried to sell things, a variety of things, over the years. The only problem was that it wasn't in line with who I was. I didn't feel aligned, so I didn't put in the effort consistently over time. Feeling aligned is KEY. Fast forward to now, I have a therapy and coaching business. These are in line with me. To my core, I love to help others directly through coaching and counseling. These are in line with me as a person and thus I've enjoyed the benefits of helping people directly. Now I realize a brick and mortar business is not for everybody. I have one physical office and a virtual business. Sometimes you have to try to find out what is and what is not for you. They say there are no failures, only lessons. Now try to learn something about yourself today!

O is for Ohm. This could be the sound you make when you meditate daily. I wanted to take a whole section out here to focus on meditation. Now when I say meditation I'm not specifying what type, whether it's sitting, yoga or tai chi. I'm just doing something to connect with my spiritual self and slow down for a few minutes each day. I started with meditation at the age of six years old. At the beginning and end of every martial arts class we'd meditate, together as a class. As a result, I learned to clear my mind and focus. In that sense karate's meditation is a mindfulness exercise. You can arrange to meditate any number of ways. I've used it specifically for sleep, focus, and when too many thoughts are flooding in. Money or abundance meditations can also be used when you are focused on your business. I currently practice yoga in the morning to help with mindfulness. Try something new or go back to what you know you like but you just haven't been doing it.

A refers to action steps to goals that must be defined. Yes, it's important to plan out your action steps but it is equally important not to get overwhelmed by the process. Just do a little at a time and you will be making progress toward your goal. Celebrate each step along the way. I find that if I don't try to wrap my head around a WHOLE PROCESS at once then I'm more likely to take the little steps I need to in order to carry forward momentum. And you're doing awesome! Keep going! (Finish this chapter!) Did you ever notice that the encouraging things you say to others are the things you need to hear yourself? Speak it out loud! It's about progress, not perfection. That's another pitfall, perfectionism. Notice when you are doing it, being a perfectionist, then let it go and do what needs to be done, imperfect as it may be.

L is for lay out steps, schedule, and track. This is only to be done when you have a FULL commitment to your goal. Be creative, I've made board games, vision boards and visual aids to help me get and stay focused. You get to show yourself *I'm the type of person who would make a chart and complete it each day*. Or *I'm planning a trip overseas with what I earn*. We often do what we feel we have to and may not look to the bigger, brighter goal. I know I'm serious when I start making to-do lists each evening for the following day.

S for spirituality is key. I've heard it said that, "all growth is spiritual growth." (Kain Ramsey) The more I get into these topics, the more I think it's true. If I fail and am not successful it probably means that I'm not growing as a person. I don't have the next thing I want because I have not yet grown into the person who has that thing (a second house by the beach). The mindfulness practices are certainly spiritual. It may provide you with a quiet moment to reflect and note where you're at mentally, emotionally, and yes, spiritually. This all sounded ludicrous to me at first, but the more I learn and look into it, I can't deny there is truth to the spiritual side of this. We are all on a spiritual journey, whether you care to notice or not is up to you. You can grow, everyone is capable of personal growth, but some people are more intentional about it. Be intentional and with the right guidance, you've got this!

In conclusion, the stigma for mental health is BS. (Right?!) Do not be ashamed if you need help; we all do at times. Secondly, you can have what you want eventually if you are willing to stretch and change into a better version of you. The M.I.N.D.G.O.A.L.S. system outlines steps to take and areas to be aware of in order to be happier today and remain on track for a better tomorrow. I am your mindgoals coach, black belt and licensed psychotherapist who was a new mama not too long ago myself. If you become a one on one client with me, I will have you break a board to symbolize you breaking out of what has held you back from pursuing your dreams in life! It's a powerful exercise that can leave you feeling truly empowered. As for the process of going from working mom to mompreneur - I would love to guide you!

About the Author

Kelsy Anderson Hoerauf is a Mindgoals Coach, Psychotherapist and badass. She loves helping women, especially new moms, to experience more happiness in life through mindfulness practices, and more time at home with the baby. Kelsy provides support and guidance as she takes the leap from exhausted, stressed employee to energized, empowered entrepreneur. Using the mindgoals approach, she helps new moms learn how to break through barriers (think wooden board!) both real and in their minds. Most powerfully, she uses her own experiences with mental health, being a mom and her relationship struggles to better understand and help clients. Her ten years of experience as a therapist and over twenty as a martial artist equip her to assist her clients in focusing on their strengths, increasing balance and kicking butt!

Website: www.peaceservicespc.com
Facebook: @kelsyandersonhoerauf
Instagram: @kelsyhboss
Facebook Group:
www.facebook.com/groups/kelsysbadasscoaching
Email: kelsy@peaceservicespc.com

Helping Ambitious Women Breakthrough Their Limitations & Live Their True Potential

By Suzanne James

If you'd have told me five years ago that I would be CEO of my own business, a Motivational Speaker, a No.1 Best Selling Author, and a Master Coach, training and coaching fab ladies around the world on how to remove their self-sabotaging limiting beliefs and live the life of their dreams, I would have laughed in your face…!

I've always been a strong-minded, driven, determined, and independent girl who liked to be in control. This is what led to numerous arguments with my mom when I was younger, who was just as strong-minded as me!

It was this that filled me with guilt when she died – why had we wasted so much time on petty little arguments?

My mom died when I was twenty-six, she was forty-seven years old. I had just got engaged and within fifteen months I experienced what they say are the top-most stressful situations in a person's life.

I got engaged, lost my mom, moved into my first home (leaving my dad and brother in our family home), got married and then had my daughter. What should have been the most fantastic times of my life, was tainted by the huge grief I felt at losing my mom.

I could easily have sunk at that time – and there were many times where I got close. Probably what I didn't realise then was actually, when faced with such powerful, life-changing events and circumstances, we can surprise ourselves. We find an inner fire, strength and courage deep inside of us. I realised just how strong I am. I had my daughter and was newly married – they were my life and that was my focus now.

I was surrounded by many family and friends at that time who were content with 'just getting by' and settling for things. I always wanted more and knew deep down I would get it.

I wasn't particularly outstanding at school and didn't do A-levels. That wasn't the thing you did in the area I went to school. I was in my twenties when I went back to college, baby in tow, to complete a HR degree.

One of the beliefs I carried with me for years (pretty much all of my HR career if I'm honest), was I wasn't good enough as I didn't have the same academic background as my peers; I wasn't as qualified, I felt a fraud, often wondering when would I be caught out. That constant self-doubt, confident on the outside but not on the inside. Feeling inadequate even though the evidence was to the contrary. I would always do way more to overcompensate and put so much pressure on myself.

My HR and Training career really started to get off the ground when I'd completed my degree. Also, by this time I'd had my son. I quickly rose through the ranks and took on a senior role in an over one-thousand employee company. It was part-time, home-based with travel across the UK. It was actually my dream job!

The role gave me the seniority and status I craved and also the flexibility to bring up my young family too.

I felt so lucky and thankful.

However, I also felt like I had to be superwoman. I had to do everything. I made sure I was at Sports Day, assemblies, reading with the children at school, as well as travelling the country with my job.

'I can do it all,' I thought.

After a couple of years in the job, desperately pleasing work and family, I suddenly started experiencing horrendous migraines. They became the bane of my life.

I was a confident, successful female in a high-level corporate role one minute and then lying in bed, in a darkened room for three days the next.

I worked in a male-dominated environment, and felt the perception was still 'she can't be as high a level as the men – having children and being part-time'. It left me feeling vulnerable. I became a people-pleaser still with that ongoing feeling I wasn't as good as them, constantly having to prove myself at that level. So, I put even more effort in, burning myself out, experiencing constant health niggles and suffering migraines every three weeks.

One thing that I have found is no matter how high up the ladder you go, you can still be filled with self-doubt, lack confidence and be overly self-critical, leading to feelings of fearfulness and anxiety, generally creating a life full of stress. I felt like a fraud and I was blagging my way through! (I have since discovered the term for this is 'imposter syndrome' and that even the most famous celebrities experience it, which weirdly makes me feel better). I was also a perfectionist (an area I still have to work on); I set high standards, putting even more pressure on myself, which led to more stress, overwhelm and frustration.

To everyone else, I was always the one smiling; always happy, always nice, always positive - but all I was doing was bottling things in. I'd learned to control my emotions when my mom died, to not let my guard down and not show vulnerability, because that's a weakness isn't it? Even watching a sad film, I'd fight to hold my tears in, as I couldn't possibly let anyone see me get upset.

The Turning Point

My own thinking shifted the minute I read the book The Secret. The whole concept of the law of attraction and manifestation has captured my heart. As a hugely positive person it totally resonates with me and I believe it guides me now (it also fits nicely with NLP).

I delved into the world of Neuro Linguistic Programming (NLP) in 2012. I was looking at enhancing my own role and developing an in-house coaching programme for employees. I'm passionate about developing and transforming people and so initially I went on a corporate training for NLP and my intrigue and curiosity started into this fascinating subject.

Soon after, I decided to see an NLP Coach myself. When I saw my coach it was like opening Pandora's box. I did not know then how the mind and body are interlinked. Using Time Line therapy™ and other NLP techniques, she was able to clear up the negative emotions and blocks I'd been bottling up since the death of my mom in 1997 and gave me tools to deal with the fear and anxiety at work. The results were quick. I actually had never experienced anything like it and couldn't believe what I was seeing. I was mesmerised by the subject and the work that she had done with me.

So much so, I immediately started studying NLP. I went through the full NLP Certification programme right from NLP Practitioner to a Certified NLP and Time Line Therapy™ Trainer and Master Coach. Nothing has transformed my life more than undertaking these trainings (and I've attended a few in my time!) It was truly amazing and life-changing.

One of the learnings from this training centred around looking after *me*. I'd totally neglected myself and I just hadn't realised the extent this can actually have on our own health and wellbeing. Simple really – we're actually no use to anyone if we're broken and burnt out. I'd always wondered why on an aeroplane safety demonstration they tell you to sort your own oxygen out first before helping anyone else. The reality is you can't help anyone if you're unconscious!

I researched comprehensively alternative ways to help with my own health to combine with my newly rejuvenated mindset work. I cut out caffeine, took turmeric and co-enzyme Q10 supplement, I created a green juice recipe (drop me a note if you'd like the recipe) that I drink every morning and re-started a yoga routine. This regime combined with releasing my negative emotions from the past, my NLP training and developing a sound mindset attitude has meant that I have not experienced a migraine in at least six years. Now if I have health niggles, I wonder what it is my body is trying to tell me or for me to pay attention to (I strongly believe that physical symptoms are a result of our thoughts and our mindset).

My career went from strength to strength. When undertaking the Master Practitioner training, I got super clear on what I wanted and allowed myself to think big. I set my goals for a six-figure salary, director-level role, having an office locally with three staff.

Within a month of completing the training course, I was offered this exact role.

The great thing about the personal breakthrough sessions within the training was it cleared my limitations and freed up the 'space in my head' to uplevel to be able to take on the new role.

I started as HR Director, the role I'd manifested, some six months later. It was the icing on the cake for everything I'd worked so hard for throughout my career.

But the excitement of getting the job didn't last long. I loved what I did but reaching the 'top' wasn't everything I thought it would be. Whilst I felt the satisfaction of achieving the goal that I'd worked so hard to get and loved, it didn't quite live up to everything I'd dreamed about. I'd got the recognition and status and that was it!

Something gnawed away at me. I knew I had a true calling to help others transform their lives like I had. By this time I had started coaching and mentoring, assisting others to get unstuck and remove their internal blocks stopping them moving forward and stepping up to their next level (on the side of my 'real' job).

I began teaching others how to do what I'd done and transforming their lives too. I set up Dare 2 Succeed Ltd offering NLP Certified Training courses and coaching services. I did all this whilst holding down my FT senior corporate job.

I wanted to go on my own. Though I started to listen to my gut, heart and intuition I still wasn't completely ready to make that BIG leap of faith. I was scared.

I was the breadwinner.

How could I even think of being that selfish? Doing things just for me. Giving up a secure highly paid job on a whim.

But it became like an itch that wouldn't go away.

Suzanne, how long are you going to wait?

And then I reached the age that my mom was when she died - Just forty-seven. And that was the big awakening.

Reaching the age my mom was when she died was my lightbulb moment to pull my finger out and stop messing around. I couldn't actually comprehend dying right now. I still had so much to do! The realisation that my mom never got to fulfil all her dreams forced me forward. It was a rude awakening to just do what makes your heart sing.

When changes started happening in my company and an opportunity came up for redundancy, I saw it as a sign and took it with both hands.

I knew the right time had come.

I decided to take the big, bold step of giving up my high-flying corporate role and set up my business – overnight I became a female entrepreneur!

I was giving up the security of a monthly pay cheque and it was seriously petrifying, let me tell you!

It would have been so much easier to go find another corporate role, but I knew in my heart that it wasn't an option.

I wanted to fulfil my passion.

I wanted to inspire and empower women to breakthrough their limitations, and transform their lives like I'd experienced, getting the success, wealth, happiness and abundance they deserved.

The reality is, your mindset affects everything you do in life. I'd seen it in my career how women still hold themselves back with the stuff that goes on in their mind. Mindset is everything and if we can change our mind, we can change our life.

I went all out with Dare 2 Succeed Ltd, continuing to run

Internationally Accredited NLP Practitioner and Master Practitioner programmes for those aspiring coaches, coaches looking to add practical NLP techniques to their belt and for those looking to transform their own lives.

And then, Suzanne James Global was born in 2019, where I launched online Coaching and Mentoring programmes and Masterminds.

I know there are high achieving women in business that have got that fire bubbling inside of them too. Having dreams, knowing there's more to life, wanting huge abundance and to be able to step into their true potential, but they're stuck, they're settling. The lack of confidence and self-belief in themselves is holding them back.

Success is an inside job – you will only take action if you believe what you're working towards is possible for you. So, it's essential to build your confidence, a positive way of thinking, belief and courage so that you have a strong foundation to build from.

My 12-week programme, 'Mega Success Mindset Accelerator' – which combines Coaching and Mentoring, alongside an online Self-Study Academy, and deeper NLP and Time Line Therapy™ techniques to reprogramme the mind for success - helps ambitious, female entrepreneurs to rapidly fast track their success in their life and business; transforming their mindset, raising their game, so they make more money and step into the life they dream of.

I developed this programme for like-minded, driven women who still have mental blocks holding them back and where their limiting beliefs sabotage themselves and keep them small. They're desperate to remove these limitations and upgrade to the next level of success, wealth and abundance. It's a three-step process with some serious up-levelling, stretching them out of their comfort zone!

I get hugely involved in the programme, getting to know each person deeply. Together we uncover the root cause of what's stopping them achieving what they want, clear the obstacles and then create the future they've longed for.

And the great thing is, during my programme these fabulous ladies are surrounded by other fabulous ladies who have the dream like them and have the same challenges as them, and together with the support from the group, and the intensive group coaching calls and implementation sessions, they achieve results beyond anything they can get on their own.

They can also upgrade to the VIP option and have additional intensive personal one to one coaching from me to accelerate their growth and financial success.

I have found my true purpose. This is what I live and breathe for. This is what I'm meant to do. Knowing that I've contributed to transforming someone's life, enabling them to live the life they dreamed about, free of limitations and completely stepping into who they are meant to be, is absolutely priceless. I'm still so shocked by how powerful this stuff is and how it can genuinely change people's lives.

I absolutely believe that everyone has the potential inside of them to do whatever they want to do. Sometimes it just needs a gentle push to bring it to the surface. I also believe that if something is important enough to us, we will move mountains to do it. Some people take the risk and pursue their dreams, others use excuses and end up in the same place, time and again, running their own treadmill of life! Constantly on the go but not moving very far!

It's not all plain sailing…

I'll be totally honest and admit that making the transition from being an employee to CEO has been tough! I've had to really draw on my inner strength and my NLP toolkit to shift my mindset.

Instead of just having one area to focus on, suddenly I've had to do finance, accounts, marketing, sales, and admin! I had to develop strategy and vision, planning and business development. As well as managing my own time effectively. I was so used to being in a structured environment with clear deadlines. And OMG don't get me talking about social media platforms, lead generation, click funnels and active campaign! I'm not going to lie – it was challenging. I was working in my business rather than on my business. I couldn't shake off the employee mindset. I had serious identity issues; having had the high-level director job I then struggled with not having that title, responsibility and recognition. I found it difficult to now answer when asked what I did for a living, I couldn't say I was the CEO - ridiculous (I know that now.) I actually felt stupid saying I ran my own business. The old stories of self-worth and belief reared their ugly heads.

I wasted so much time in my business constantly trying to figure out what to do next instead of planning effectively. I was juggling everything in the air. It took a while to work this out! I had to find a system to work smarter instead of working harder. I had days of not knowing what the hell I was doing, drifting from one thing to another, feeling the scarcity mindset, feeling guilty for placing my family at risk – I was the breadwinner so what the heck did I think I was doing. My son was going off to university and yet there I was giving up a secure job with great money! How would we afford it?

And actually, I couldn't do it on my own (or rather I could have done but I wasn't prepared to wait years to do it!) I wanted it right now, so I sought help from someone already doing what I wanted to do. I joined a Mentorship programme in 2019 to create serious momentum in my business. This was a huge investment at a time of insecurity. But I trusted in it. I wasn't playing small anymore. And I've continued to invest heavily in myself, joining a business mastermind and having a business coach. I believe so passionately in the benefits of having a coach myself.

And do you know what – I love it!

I have the freedom to do whatever I choose to do. I'm the healthiest, fittest and happiest I've ever been. I have 'healthy stress' now – the type that motivates me and continually drives me forward. I can relax on holiday without being phoned to deal with a drama or answering emails in the middle of a family meal. I never compromise on family time. I made a promise to myself early on that I would have a holiday or short break away every twelve weeks and I've stuck to that. I make sure that I do stuff for me – I have my non-negotiables like exercising and looking after myself; having my hair done every six weeks; my nails done every three weeks. I'm designing my own life exactly as I want it.

I've learnt to not compare myself to others, to be kind to myself, to not worry what other people think, to let go of the need to be perfect, that showing vulnerability is okay, to give myself a pat on the back and remember how far I have come (and it's usually a hell of a lot more than we give ourselves credit for) to trust in the Universe, to trust in myself, and forever be grateful for everything that I have in my life.

I continue to invest in my own self-development and to me that's key. How can I expect others to invest in themselves if I don't invest in me?

I use NLP and Mindset skills and my toolkit of techniques every day in my life. I have an overriding passion for seeing people develop and NLP does just that. There is nothing better than seeing the personal transformation in people and knowing that you've been a part of that and assisted them to live the life they want to lead, free of the limitations that have held them back in the past. I get a real buzz seeing the impact my coaching has on women's lives.

Some quick simple tips for being the best you!

- Take 100% responsibility for your own life. Regardless of anything that is happening outside of us, we all have the ability to create the life we want. Everything about you is a result of your doing or not doing. You're the one driving your own bus. Successful people take full responsibility for the thoughts they think and the actions they take. They don't waste time and energy blaming and complaining. Life isn't what happens to you – you are creating it and knowing this is hugely empowering.

- The ONLY person getting in your way and stopping you living the life you want is YOU. Just stop it! Get a coach who can help you clear up your stuff and get rid of those limitations holding you back. You can't do this on your own. It is not a weakness to ask for help from those who know what they're doing, it's a strength.

- Decide what you truly want (most people know what they don't want but find it more challenging to articulate exactly what they do want). Focus on what you do want and what's important to you– focus on opportunities, not obstacles. *Energy flows where your focus goes* so make sure you're directing your energy right.

- Enjoy the journey. It's all about the ride. Envision your life already as you want it to be – In the morning, visualise your day as if it's already happened. It gives so much satisfaction knowing you're the creator of your day.

- Use positive language to yourself and others (cut out the 'I can't' and replace with 'I can').

- Take action - JFDI is now my motto! I spent so much time worrying about what others would think or trying to perfect everything (in case I failed or actually in case I was successful) and all it did was stop me moving forward. There is no right time so JFDI now!

- Believe in yourself - Believe you can achieve whatever you desire and set your mind to. You can never get to a place you don't believe exists.

- If you really want a better life, stop making excuses. Stop letting your past define who you are.

- Think BIG and Dream BIG – stop settling for average or a life of okay. Set HUGE goals, DREAM BIG, go after that abundance. Stretch yourself. Remember the saying, 'Shoot for the moon, because even if you miss, you land among the stars'. Dare to dream the so-called impossible and it will really open up the possibilities to you. The brain loves repetition of thoughts; by looking at options of how you can achieve crazy big goals, your brain becomes accustomed to the idea and the goal doesn't seem so impossible anymore.

I'm now really proud of the person I've become and how I've used my life experiences to drive me forward in my life and business. I know my mom would be proud too and I know she's looking down on me guiding me. I feel her everywhere.

My children are following in my footsteps too – I can see the same drive, determination, positivity and hunger for success. My daughter started her own dance company in 2019 at just twenty years old! My son started his degree in accountancy and he's already talking about being my finance director!

Our past shapes who we are today but we should never let it dictate our future. Life is way too short. Never be afraid to pursue your dreams…

Suzanne James
NLP Trainer and Female Success Coach

Apply to work with me – www.calendly.com/suzannej-25/success-accelerator-session

To find out more about my 'Mega Success Mindset Accelerator' visit - www.suzannejamesglobal.com/the-accelerator
To learn more about my NLP Certification Programmes – www.dare2succeed.co.uk

About the Author

Suzanne James is a Female Success Coach, a Certified NLP and Time Line Therapy™ Trainer and Master Coach. She's on a mission to inspire and empower thousands of women across the world to abandon their limitations, rise up, live their best life and step into their true potential. She gave up her corporate HR Director job to follow her passion and now helps women to transform their lives and take their life and business to the next level. They gain the confidence and self-belief to get the success and five-figure month income they truly desire, by removing those self-sabotaging behaviours at the deeper unconscious level with techniques to reprogram the mind.

Website: www.suzannejamesglobal.com and www.dare2succeed.co.uk
Facebook Page: www.facebook.com/SuzanneJamesGlobal
Facebook Group:
www.facebook.com/groups/BossBabeOnTheRise
for Money, Mindset, Motivation for the Ambitious Woman!
Instagram: @suzannejamesglobal
Email: Suzanne@suzannejamesglobal.com

Happiness is Possible

By Jo Howarth

My life officially fell apart when I was twenty-five.

I remember the phone call as if it was yesterday and yet it was almost twenty-five years ago now. I was living in a shared house with some friends. I was on the dole because at the time I wanted to be a world-famous actress, except I didn't have the confidence or self-belief to actually go to auditions, so I spent most of my time 'resting' whilst watching television.

On this particular afternoon, I was watching a TV show, curled up on my armchair, perfectly at peace with the world, when the phone rang. I got up to answer it, mobile phones didn't exist in those days, and it was my mum.

She was calling to tell me that my biological dad, they had split when I was five years old, had died of a heart attack. No signs, no symptoms, no warning, just gone.

At first, I misunderstood. I thought she meant her dad so I started telling her how sorry I was and how much I would miss my lovely grandad. But as she continued talking, the penny dropped. She was talking about my dad, MY dad. He was fifty years old. There one day, gone the next. And in that instant, my world turned upside down, inside out and back to front.

The following few months were a blur. My biggest memory is thinking that nothing mattered anymore. In fact, that became my mantra, "it doesn't matter". All these things that I used to think were important were suddenly completely unimportant. All these things that used to wind me up or upset me just didn't matter anymore.

I was lost. I barely knew how to put one foot in front of the other and I didn't have a clue where I was going or what I was doing when I got there. Grief would overwhelm me at any moment and I would be in floods of tears. I felt guilty for laughing, ashamed of having fun. It all seemed so wrong.

Then one day, about a month after my dad left us, I went for a walk in the sunshine with a friend of mine. She had been having therapy for a while and she told me that she had spoken to her therapist about me. She had told him what a dark place I was in and he told her that I needed to go and see him.

Up until that point, I thought that any kind of counselling or therapy was a load of bumkum, utter codswallop. If you couldn't bury whatever you needed to bury inside you and carry on regardless, then you weren't worth the paper you were written on. But the moment she said those words I knew she was right, that her therapist was right; I needed help because I was lost.

A few weeks later I turned up for my first ever therapy session, determined not to give too much away, determined not to show him what a fuck-up I was.

This wonderful man started the session by asking me this question: "So, tell me, Jo, what is wrong with you?"

I started to reel off a list of all the things that I thought were wrong with me as a person. He held his hand up gently to stop the words that were tumbling out of my mouth and said, "Can I tell you the answer?"

Nervously, I nodded in agreement.

"Nothing. There is nothing wrong with you. You've simply picked up some beliefs that aren't doing you any favours and we can sort those out for you."

With those words, I felt the most tremendous wave of relief flood through my body and I began to cry. I had spent so much of my life feeling wrong, as if I was broken in some way. I had spent my whole life hiding how I really felt and what I really thought because I believed nobody would love me if they knew how awful

I was. And here was this man telling me it was all okay and that I didn't need to feel like this anymore.

I stayed in therapy for a couple of years. My therapist, Eamonn, helped me to release so many of the subconscious beliefs that were holding me back in life. Beliefs that I had largely learnt as a young child, beliefs that were handed to me by the adults around me and by the situations I had been involved in.

We looked at the trauma I had experienced when my parents split, and it IS a traumatic event for anyone involved in the break-up of a marriage. At the tender age of five my family unit had been taken away from me. I don't consciously remember any of it but, knowing what I know now about how important those early years of childhood are for our development, I know it had an enormous impact on my self-esteem, my confidence and my beliefs about myself and the world around me.

After my parents split, my dad re-married and my mum got a new partner. To say that my mum and stepdad's relationship was turbulent would be an understatement; they were both injured people, people that were hurt and hurting and they took that out on each other a lot of the time. My stepdad was rather fond of an alcoholic drink, especially when he was feeling down. My overwhelming memory, when it comes to my childhood, was one of fear, of being scared all the time.

I learnt very quickly to walk on eggshells, to do my best not to get noticed, to not rock the boat in any way if I could possibly help it. I spent a lot of my childhood curled up on my bed with my head in a book; it was pure escapism for me, leaving the reality of life and entering into all kinds of amazing worlds in my head.

All of those experiences gave me one hell of a set of self-limiting subconscious beliefs. My therapist definitely had his work cut out for him!

Over time he helped me to transform my life, to release those beliefs and replace them with more positive ones, to start seeing the world for the wonderful, amazing thing that it is and myself for the wonderful, amazing thing that I am too.

At the time that my dad passed away I was also embroiled in an emotionally abusive relationship. I didn't know it was that until I began therapy; my partner treated me in the same kind of way as the adults from my childhood had treated me, so whilst a lot of the time it was horrible to experience, it was also 'normal' for me. As my beliefs changed and my confidence grew, I began to accept that treatment less and less. I began to put boundaries in place for myself; I began to treat myself with more love and respect. And I began to realise that this relationship was all kinds of wrong. The whole thing came to a head one horrible day when my partner raped me. I don't know exactly why that happened. I don't know if it had always been likely or if he could feel me changing and wanted to assert his authority, to make me 'his' again.

I do know that I have never felt so ashamed in my whole life. We didn't speak about it afterwards and I stayed with him for months after it had happened, mostly because I blamed myself and partly because I didn't want to admit that it had actually happened.

I held that shame and blame inside me for almost twenty years before I finally went back to my therapist about it. I hadn't felt able to talk about it at all when I first had therapy, it got buried very deep.

But even with that shame buried inside, I continued to grow and develop as a person. I continued to do the inner work to release all those old beliefs and emotions. I continued to put down the stuff from my past, to commit to not carrying it forward with me in my life any further.

I moved through a couple more relationships, one with an alcoholic, mirroring the things I had experienced as a child and then I met my husband-to-be.

I was twenty-nine. I had changed so much over the years of having therapy. I was still shy and lacking in confidence, I was still experiencing the anxiety that had been with me throughout most of my childhood, but I had taken so many steps forward and released so much unwanted stuff.

I had given up trying to be a world-famous actress by this point and got a 'proper' job working in event management. I organised conferences, exhibitions and awards dinners with a team of people at the marketing agency that employed us all. And it was at that agency that I met my future husband.

We were polar opposites, but we connected deeply. Within a couple of months of dating I knew that we were a family. I knew that this was the man I would marry and have children with. It took us another five years to get there, but I knew so quickly.

Becoming a mummy was everything that I had ever wanted. I had wanted my own children for as long as I could remember; I was ready to have kids, I was ready to have my own family.

The reality of having two children under two years old was somewhat harder than I thought it would be. I had given up work to become a full-time mum and I struggled to cope with the lack of sleep, the lack of energy and the emotions it brought to the surface for me.

When my eldest daughter was about four years old, I went running back to therapy. I knew that I was becoming the kind of parent that I had experienced as a child and I did not want that for my beautiful children. I was in my late thirties, I wasn't working, I had everything that I had thought I wanted, and I still wasn't happy in myself.

During those therapy sessions, we uncovered more limiting beliefs from my childhood and I became a calmer, happier mummy, more able to cope with the pressures of that lifestyle. But I also realised that I needed to find something to do with my life apart from being a mum.

I started asking my therapist more about his work and how to do what he did for people. I asked him if he thought I would be suitable and capable for that kind of work. He looked at me and said, "Jo, I've been waiting ten years for you to ask me that."

We both smiled and so my training to become an advanced hypnotherapist began with the man who had helped me change my life all those years ago.

During our year of training in hypnotherapy I also discovered the amazing practice of mindfulness through an event I was involved in organising. One of the speakers was a mindfulness teacher. This quiet, unassuming man took to the stage for fifteen minutes and totally blew my mind. I knew in that instant that I had to learn everything I could about this practice, and I knew that he had to teach me.

So, within the space of a year, I went from being a stay-at-home mum, doing occasional freelance event work, to being a qualified advanced hypnotherapist and mindfulness practitioner.

That was almost nine years ago and my business journey has been interesting. I have continued to do the inner work, to grow and develop. I wholeheartedly believe that there is always growth. In

Dreamers & Change Makers

fact, I believe that's what we are here to do, to learn and grow and develop and expand ourselves because as we do that work, we expand the world around us too.

Over those years I have come to realise that everything is an experience. Every situation, every issue, every difficulty, every challenge, every joy, every moment. All of it is there for us to experience so that we may develop and expand. Every last little bit of it gives us something, whether we feel it at the time or not. It is all an experience that is here for us to experience.

Understanding that has allowed me to let go of so much stuff. Understanding that has softened the impact of those 'negative' situations, to the point where I no longer see them as negative. In fact, I no longer believe in negative emotions. All of our emotions are there to tell us something, to give us a message of some kind, to help us. Some of those emotions aren't particularly pleasant to experience, they don't feel very nice, but they are always trying to guide us towards whatever it is that we want.

I know now that without all of those earlier experiences I wouldn't be the person I am today, doing the work that I do and love, helping the people I help and living the life that I adore. Each one of those experiences helped me to learn and grow, to move forward in some way. I wouldn't be without a single one of them now, I simply wouldn't be who I am without them.

We learn how to be as human beings through the experiences we have when we are young, I have no doubt about that. We are taught how to be, we are shaped, we are programmed and conditioned.

I want you to take a moment to imagine a pair of Wellington boots, you know, the rubber boots you wear to go and splash in puddles. I want you to imagine you have just bought yourself a brand spanking new pair of wellies. They are clean and shiny, in your favourite colour. You bring those boots home and decide to go out for a walk across the fields in them, so you pull them on and off you go. As you walk in the muddy fields, obviously those boots get mud on them but you carry on walking until you get back home then you put them by the back door and carry on with your day.

The next day, you decide to do some gardening so on go the boots and outside you go, digging and weeding and getting more mud on those boots. And the next day you decide to go walking in the fields again and you get more mud and more mud and more mud on your wellies.

After a few days, you look at your boots sitting by the back door and you realise that you can't even see what colour they are anymore, all you can see is mud. Your boots are covered in mud. So, you decide to take them outside and wash them down. You get the hose pipe on them and start scrubbing. Some of that mud comes off easily, some of it takes a bit of scrubbing and some of it needs a lot of scrubbing but eventually, your boots are almost like new again, clean and shiny once more.

Why am I telling you about wellies? Because I believe we are the same. I believe we come into this world as pure, positive, beautiful, shiny energy. And as we walk through life we experience things and some of those things cover us in 'mud'. The mud of those limiting beliefs, the mud of that learnt behaviour. Sometimes the mud completely covers up the fact that we are that pure, positive energy and the bit that breaks my heart the most is that we start to believe that we are the mud. We start to believe that who we actually are is the mud of those thoughts and beliefs. But we aren't, we are the wellies underneath that mud. Who we truly are is that beautiful, pure, positive energy. And we can absolutely wash that mud off if we choose to.

One of the most beautiful paths of my life has been uncovering my true self, chipping the mud of those earlier experiences off and remembering who I really am. It seems to be a paradox to me that the things I learnt as a child are what led me to the path that helped me to unlearn those things and discover who I truly am. Love.

That is what we are really made of. Love. Each and every one of us. We come from love, we are here to give and receive love, and we return to love.

In each and every moment we have a choice: love or fear. We have become more used to choosing fear. We find it easier to choose fear, whatever that looks like. Sometimes fear looks like anger, sometimes like panic, sometimes like violence. We have learnt how to be fearful, we have learnt how to integrate fear into our lives.

We stop ourselves from experiencing joy, out of fear. We stop ourselves from doing the things we want, out of fear. We stop ourselves from achieving the things we want to achieve, out of fear.

Yet the choice is there: love or fear. We always have the option to choose love over fear. We always have the option to respond with love instead of fear. Always.

And that is where true happiness lies. In knowing that everything is happening for you, not to you. In understanding that everything is happening in order that you can experience it, so that you can grow. In knowing that, regardless of what is happening, you can always choose love instead of fear. In understanding that you are the wellies, you are not the mud.

I am living proof that it is possible to find happiness no matter where you come from or what you have experienced in your life. Please know that whatever you are going through, whatever you are facing right now, you can and will come out the other side.

Please know that happiness is possible.

About the Author

Jo Howarth is an Advanced Hypnotherapist and Mindfulness Practitioner. She runs The Happiness Club and she teaches people how to look after their mental health and emotional wellbeing. She is happily married to Trev, has two beautiful daughters and two gorgeous cats.

The Happiness Club is a monthly membership club where members receive daily support from and 24/7 access to qualified therapists.

Jo also works with corporate organisations that are committed to supporting their employees. She works within schools to teach students techniques to develop their own resilience and she has a team of Happiness Club Trainers that deliver her training to corporates and schools across the world.

Jo is an inspirational speaker, advanced hypnotherapist, mindfulness practitioner and bestselling author of four books. In 2017 she won two national awards for her work in The Happiness Club and in 2020 she was runner-up for North West Entrepreneur of the Year, the only female finalist.

Website: www.thehappinessclub.co.uk

Facebook Page: www.facebook.com/TheHappinessClubLtd

Facebook Group: www.facebook.com/groups/456685845077201

Email: jo@thehappinessclub.co.uk

From Broken Single Mom, To Travelling The World: How Changing Your Thoughts Can Change Your Life

By Amoya Shante

I sat on the cold bathroom floor as a broken woman. My worst fear had come true and my life had changed overnight. I was a single mom again. My dreams of staying home with my youngest, who was only three-months-old at the time and taking a year off school to be with her before going to graduate school, were crushed. All I could see ahead of me was the all too familiar life of struggle as a single mom.

How could this have happened again? I did everything 'right' this time. I got married, finished the degree, bought the house in the picture-perfect neighborhood with the cheery neighbor named Bob. Yet, here I was in a tiny condo on the other side of town, crying on the bathroom floor.

My kids needed me, but I could barely care for myself, much less a newborn and an eight- and nine-year-old. I failed them for many reasons. The first being that I didn't get out of that abusive marriage sooner. The second being that I allowed myself to stay for so many years in the first place, despite all the red flags.

Over the next few months, I would spend a lot of time in bed. Life felt pointless and if I am being completely honest, I didn't want to live. Every day was a battle with myself to find the will to continue living for my girls' sake.

One of our go-to dishes was nachos because that is all I could find the strength to make for them. Tortilla chips, shredded cheddar cheese, put in the oven for 30 minutes, and voila!

The dish actually became rather comforting despite its lack of nutrition. We watched a lot of Netflix and the girls missed a lot of school because they too were struggling from the loss. Sometimes getting them to school early on those cold mornings seemed an impossible act so instead, we stayed home in bed watching TV together letting our sadness get lost in our favorite shows.

Their school started getting upset with me. I was called into the office one day and told that if my middle child could not pass the end of year test, she would be held back a grade. All I could think about was the fact that our family was suffering and all these people were concerned with was my daughter passing a test. One test would determine if she could go to the next grade.

I left angry and found myself at home searching YouTube trying to learn about home-schooling. There had to be a different option than sending my kids to a school that only cared about testing and not the actual emotional well-being of a child.

A video on unschooling and world-schooling caught my eye. It was a TED Talk by Lanie Liberti and her son Miro. I'd never heard of either term before, but I was instantly pulled in by the joy they exuded from the stage. They'd been traveling the world for years while learning about the world around them. It was so radical, yet so intriguing at the same time. A life of travel. A life of learning from actual life instead of solely from a curriculum and books. I could feel a sense of freedom coming through the screen.

Still... I was a single mom, could barely afford the rent on my condo, was still in the process of selling my marital home across town, the divorce was not finalized and the lawyer bills were stacking up. Plus, I was a broken woman.

It would be a few more weeks of taking my kids to school before a crazy idea over Valentine's Day came to me. We needed a little 'vacay.' I jumped on Airbnb and started looking at places to stay on the coast of Texas. I'd always wanted to go to the coast but never had, so why not now?

I quickly realized that it was a whole lot cheaper to travel during the week than it was to travel on the weekends. Before I knew it, I hit 'book' on a yurt near the beach in Port Aransas, Texas. It would be our first road trip since my youngest, Novella, was born. I honestly didn't know how it would go driving nearly five hours with a five-month-old but something inside me said I had to do it.

I told the girls after picking them up from school. They were so excited to skip a few days of school and go on this adventure. They needed this trip as much as I did. It was during that trip of a few days, staying in a yurt, exploring Port Aransas, that everything changed for us.

For the first time in months, we laughed. We forgot the pain and worry and we just lived. Each night we stayed up late, laying in bed talking about all kinds of things. We forgot about life back home. Instead, we woke to the morning sun slowly. We did what we wanted when we wanted. Everything was new and exciting. It was off-season so there weren't many other tourists in the tourist town which made it seem like we had the whole island to ourselves. There was a sense of peace in the air.

Our four-day trip came to an end and we made the five-hour drive back to Austin, right back into the routine of waking to an alarm and rushing the girls off to school only for me to come home and crawl back into bed with Novella until it was time to pick them up from school again.

The sadness and pain came rushing back. I felt stuck. I hit the rock bottom of all rock bottoms.

I remembered our trip to Port Aransas. I remembered the laughter, joy, and sense of adventure. I asked myself the question, "What if we could travel all the time instead of every once in a while? What if we could feel that joy and freedom all the time?"

But how? There was no way I could afford rent, a car payment, insurance, and everything else, plus travel. I thought back to that TED Talk by Lainie Liberti. At that exact moment, the craziest idea ever came to me. It was absolutely insane but also the most exciting thing I had ever thought of.

There was a way we could travel all the time. I was medically retired from the military, so I already had a location independent income. It wasn't much but it could be enough if I could eliminate all my bills and travel to countries where the cost of living was much cheaper than in Austin, Texas. If we sold all our possessions and ended the lease on our condo, we could actually make a life of travel work.

Within thirty days of that idea, I had ended the lease on our condo, pulled the girls out of school, sold all our possessions, and entered into the world of full-time travel starting with a month in Puerto Rico.

As soon as I had the idea and believed it was possible for us, everything came together so quickly. I didn't have to subscribe to the belief that just because I was a single mom, my life had to be miserable. I could live whatever life I wanted.

Puerto Rico seemed like a wise first choice since it didn't require passports; I figured as it was US territory it would be easy to navigate with just knowing English. I was very wrong.

Puerto Rico was just the introduction I needed for a life of travel and living abroad. It pushed me in ways I never could have imagined, starting with our very first week there. I booked the cheapest Airbnb I could find. It was $800 for the month; a little house in the middle of the rainforest.

I rented a car for the month figuring that driving in Puerto Rico couldn't be much different than driving in Texas. I was in for a rude awakening. As soon as our little blue rental car pulled out of the airport, I was surrounded by cars everywhere seemingly dancing with each other in a dance I was not familiar with. There were massive potholes that threatened to swallow our little rental.

My Verizon phone plan was supposed to work but I struggled to find a signal, especially after turning into the rainforest. We were losing daylight and my anxiety quickened. Surrounded by trees there was no human life for miles and miles. Thirty minutes into the rainforest, we saw burnt down cars on the side of the road almost as a warning to not go any further. Stop. Turn around. Don't look back. That's what I felt like the cars were trying to tell us.

I had no idea at this point if we were even headed in the right direction. With a lack of signal, and unable to reach the Airbnb owner, I feared we would be sleeping in our car that night or that I would eventually drive off a cliff because I couldn't see what was in front of me.

My phone caught a signal and it gave me just enough time to reach the Airbnb owner who was able to direct us to the home. A sense of relief washed over me. We pulled up to a little home surrounded by lush rainforest and a creek.

The woman showed us around the place. Everything seemed OK at first. I was just grateful we had found the place, but then I noticed there was no AC which seemed like torture with the tropical temperature of Puerto Rico. It was when she showed me the bathroom that I really got concerned. There was a giant hole in the ceiling next to the light fixture and water was dripping from it into a bucket below. She told us not to worry. She would eventually get it fixed when it stopped raining. The only issue with that was that it was the rainforest. It literally rained all the time. She also casually mentioned that we couldn't flush toilet paper; it was to go in the trash. I was absolutely appalled at this statement. The funny thing is that I would later learn during our travels that this was actually the norm in Latin America and we would grow used to it. At the time though, it was horrendous to even think about.

That night we went to sleep, sticky from all the humidity, to the sound of the rainforest.

Needless to say, we only lasted a couple of days in the house before I contacted Airbnb and explained the situation to them. They let us leave that house and move into another. I found a little air-conditioned studio right on the beach. We spent our month in Puerto Rico in that studio. It was tiny but it was completely renovated with an ocean view.

Each day we'd wake up to the morning sun and take a walk on the beach. My girls did their homework in their own time at the small brown table. We ate foods new to us, swam in the ocean, made traveling friends, and explored the cobblestone streets of Old San Juan. Navigating the language was a lot more challenging than I could have imagined. In fact, I would often shamefully drive to McDonalds for dinner because I figured there someone would speak English.

I wrote on my blog about our experiences. At first, only a few people read it. I didn't know then that two years from that trip thirty thousand people a month would be reading that little hobby blog of mine and I'd be actually making money from my writing.

One late afternoon, I started a group on Facebook called Single Moms DO Travel. I struggled to find positive single mom groups online. Every single mom group I joined was full of negativity. I wanted to connect with other single moms who were intentional in creating lives they loved, that traveled and lived abroad. Lanie and I surely couldn't have been the only ones, right?

My group started with just a few people, then a few hundred, then a few thousand until nearly eight thousand, before years later I would hand the group over to someone else so I could make my move off of Facebook.

There were so many ups and downs in Puerto Rico. It was in that country that I started to wake up to my strength. The idea that I could do whatever I wanted and live how I wanted formulated in my mind. I'd already overcome so much fear by making the leap into a life of full-time travel. Surely, this meant I could do anything.

I wasn't supported on my journey a lot of the time. People doubted me and criticized me, but I chose to not listen. I chose to live and so can you; ignore the naysayers.

What if the common narrative of single moms' lack and struggle often portrayed in society could be changed to one of empowerment and abundance? This is the idea that led me to create the Single Moms DO movement. A movement that is all about amplifying the voices of single moms all around the world and showing the world all the things single moms can do.

When you start living in your purpose it will shine a light on others. All of a sudden, all the excuses they made for why they weren't living the life they wanted will no longer hold value because they will see you doing it. This can make the people in your life highly uncomfortable. You must be able to overcome any push back and negativity thrown your way and continue living in your purpose.

Over the next four years, I traveled and lived abroad in Canada, Mexico, Northern Ireland, Italy, Albania, Kosovo, and Guatemala.

Life was tough at times, but I learned that I could choose to be happy. I could choose to live a life of ease and joy and that no one could take that from me.

I learned about the power of mindset and started showing other single moms how powerful their minds truly were.

I literally turned my passion for helping single moms overcome their limiting beliefs and create a life of freedom into a business. I'd heard of people talking about making money from their passions but for years I didn't even know what I was passionate about, much less how to turn it into a business.

I knew I loved storytelling and sharing our journey. I knew I loved inspiring single moms. I lived for the moment when someone would write to me and tell me they finally found the courage to leave their abusive marriage after reading my blog.

We all have a call to greatness. You find your calling by listening. What are you interested in? What do you absolutely love doing? What do you like to share with others? What makes you feel energized?

The Single Moms DO Movement needed a place to be cultivated, away from the distractions and noise of social media. I knew I wanted a place that didn't depend on algorithms and wasn't drowned out by the negativity that can often be found on social media.

The Single Moms DO Inner Circle membership site was born February 1st, 2020 in my single mom hostel in Merida, Mexico one month prior to the pandemic. One hundred women signed up to be part of it on its initial launch and over three hundred women joined the Inner Circle in 2020.

The women in the Inner Circle are leaders, authors, creatives, game changers, entrepreneurs, business owners, and so much more. They know that the solution to any problem starts with how you think. It starts with mindset.

They choose every day to make their dreams a reality despite all the obstacles and challenges that might be thrown their way. Excuses are left at the door where they belong.

They know that the losses and challenges they have experienced have been their greatest lessons and helped them to grow. Failures are life opportunities.

The Single Moms DO Movement has inspired thousands of single moms all around the world to take charge of their mindset and say YES to a life well-lived. This powerful movement continues to spread positivity, freedom, and hope to the lives of some of the most overlooked people in the world: single moms.

If you are struggling today, know this; you have the power within you to change your life. Sure, you might face obstacles and challenges, but the true challenge is your own thoughts and beliefs.

Take charge of those thoughts and beliefs and by doing so you will transform your life.

I could still be sitting in that tiny condo as a broken woman who blamed everyone else for the problems in my life. Luckily, I woke up to the cold hard facts that my life was the way it was because of choices I had made. If I wanted a different life, then I had to choose differently. Now, I live a life that four years ago, I could only have imagined.

Each and every day I get to do the work I love, live wherever I want, and experience freedom on levels that others can only dream of.

I believe wholeheartedly that you too can create a life of absolute freedom. Stop waiting. Stop letting fear or others' opinions hold you back from fully living the life you want to live.

Today, make the choice that no matter what, you are going to go after your dreams. If you get knocked down, you will pick yourself up and you will pick others up along the way. You owe it to yourself to live a life of purpose and meaning. Now is your chance. What are you waiting for?

About the Author

Amoya Shante is a Social Entrepreneur and Online Mindset and Manifestation Mentor for empowered single moms. She has spent the last four years traveling the world with her three daughters, building intentional communities both in-person and online, and diving deep into the world of self-development and manifestation. She is the founder of the Single Moms DO movement and has helped and inspired thousands of single moms all over the world to transform their lives. Amoya helps single moms drop their limiting beliefs, so they can manifest a life of absolute freedom.

Website: www.amoyashante.com
YouTube: (8) Amoya Shante - YouTube
Instagram: www.instagram.com/amoyashante/
Email: hello@amoyashante.com

Index

Acknowledgements

I would like to thank everyone who has purchased this book in support of our amazing charities. Our wonderful editor and copywriter Rachie, who completed the project in record time. The team who helped put the book together, including Sue, and Michelle from Team Author UK and Markie. And finally, Adriana Monique Alvarez who inspired me to launch this book and create Pineapple Publishing.

Chanel x

In deference to our global audience, we have interchanged American and US English where relevant to each author.